EXPECT
GREAT
THINGS

EXPECT
GREAT
THINGS

Mission quotes
that inform and inspire

Compiled by

MARVIN J. NEWELL

WILLIAM CAREY
LIBRARY

Expect Great Things: Mission Quotes that Inform and Inspire
Copyright © 2013 by Marvin J. Newell

Published by William Carey Library
1605 E. Elizabeth Street
Pasadena, CA 91104 | www.missionbooks.org

Kelley K. Wolfe, editor
Walter Peters, copyeditor
Hugh Pindur, graphic designer
Rose Lee-Norman, indexer

William Carey Library is a ministry of the
U.S. Center for World Mission
Pasadena, CA | www.uscwm.org

Printed in the United States of America
17 16 15 14 13   5 4 3 2 1 COU 4000

Library of Congress Cataloging-in-Publication Data
Newell, Marvin J.
  Expect great things : mission quotes that inform and inspire / complied by Marvin J. Newell.
    pages cm
  ISBN 978-0-87808-626-9
  1. Missions--Quotations, maxims, etc. I. Title.
  BV2064.N49 2013
  266--dc23
                              2013004857
  2012044576

DEDICATION

❖ ❖ ❖

This book is dedicated to the memory of William Carey (1761–1834),
known as the "Father of Modern Missions" and also
author of the most well-known mission quote
in the English language:

"Expect great things: attempt great things"

reminding us that faith-filled expectation must precede
any and all attempts on behalf of God.

❖ ❖ ❖

CONTENTS

INTRODUCTION

Through the years there have been many inspiring and insightful statements specific to the missionary task uttered by those who have known it best. The 700 quotes contained in this book bring together the best of them. Some are classical, having been given in the distant past by well-known missionaries, missionary statesmen, teachers, and preachers. Others are quite contemporary. Some are pithy one-liners that carry a meaningful punch; others are extended paragraphs that develop a thought-provoking mission theme.

THE VALUE OF QUOTES

Many have discovered good quotes to be a treasure trove of wisdom. One may go deep into the heart and mind of others by reading what they have insightfully passed along on a particular topic. Some quotes inspire, others inform, and still others educate and motivate. Some prick the heart, while others stimulate the mind. All offer nuggets of insight into something that the originator has likely, through experience, thought long and hard about. While some are more inspiring than others, all are impacting.

THE PROCESS

The searching, screening, and selecting of choice mission statements is both exciting and laborious. It is exciting in that in the midst of digging deep into mission sources, suddenly a gem, much like a "pearl of great price," is uncovered. Like panning for gold, when the effort yields a valuable reward, there is a feeling of satisfaction and an anticipation to search and find more.

The process is also laborious, as it takes time and effort to discover a quotation, reflect on its value, check to see if it is genuine, then select it as something noteworthy that others may value as well. However, this is well worth the effort. By laboring through classical and contemporary writings and then compiling them in this one volume, a ready source of quotes is available to those who do not have time to invest in such an effort.

RELIABILITY

A primary concern of anyone who quotes from another is the authenticity of the excerpt. How can we be sure it is genuine? Indeed, some quotes attributed to people of the past cannot be substantiated as having been said by them. Accordingly, this book omitted those that could not be documented as said or written by someone to whom it was attributed. Regrettably, this standard caused the screening out of some quotations that over time have become favorites.

For instance, take the quote, "The future is as bright as the promises of God." This is a wonderful quote that has been used by many. However, it is not included in this book based on the uncertainty of authorship. Research has shown that it has been attributed to both William Carey and Adoniram Judson. Therefore, the question arose, "Who was the undisputed originator of this quote?" Since it was impossible to verify to whom it should be credited, it was lamentably decided to exclude this favorite to maintain the integrity of this book. Other notable quotations were excluded on the same basis.

In order to ensure the accuracy of a quote, a "quotation criticism" method was employed. There were instances when the primary source of a quotation was not successfully uncovered. In those instances, multiple secondary sources were compared and weighed. When the preponderance of evidence pointed to the best rendering, that was the one selected.

This process determined the correct rendering of the most famous mission quote of all time—William

Carey's "Expect great things: attempt great things."
Many would prefer it to have been included in its more
popular and spiritually embellished form and the way
most of us have quoted it through the years:

> *"Expect great things from God;*
> *attempt great things for God."*

Research indicates that the former rendering was
more probably how Carey spoke it in his 1792 sermon
at the Baptist Association meeting in Northampton,
England. Thus the author has conceded to that shorter
reading. Since this quote is so popular, a helpful
explanation of its etymological history is included in
the Appendix.

SOURCES CONSULTED

Primary sources were sought for the citation of each
quotation. When that was not possible, secondary
sources were compared, and the most reliable
secondary source was used. For instance, several
websites that compile quotations were examined.
A website that originates from an educational
institution or mission agency had priority over those
that did not. Third-hand sources were discounted
altogether. These include blogs, tweets, Facebook
entries, and other popular social media outlets where

quotes are abundantly encountered. Although, when compared to a primary source, a third-party source may have recorded a mission quote correctly, its distance from the original discounted it as a viable source for inclusion in this book.

QUOTE "ORIGINATORS"

Many of the persons quoted in this book are well-known missionaries, missionary statesmen, mission leaders, mission professors, pastors, devotional writers, and even some laity. As such, they need no introduction. Others, from both the past and present, are lesser known. With few exceptions, no explanation is given in this book as to the identity of the originators. In this age when a quick Internet search would readily identify that person, the author has left it to the reader to search on his own a quote originator he may not know.

WHERE TO USE QUOTES

Perhaps you have been searching for a definitive source of inspiring mission quotations. This book gives you the most comprehensive collection ever compiled. Granted, one can find other compilations on various websites. A quick Internet search makes that clear.

But none contains the volume, documented reliability, and variety of relevant mission-related topics found in this book.

Read them for personal encouragement. Paste them on your website, blog, or other social media. Tweet them to a friend. Include them in sermons, speeches, newsletters, and lesson plans. Pass them along to others to encourage them along their way to Great Commission familiarity and commitment. "How good is a timely word" (Proverbs 15:23).

Marvin J. Newell
Senior Vice President, Missio Nexus

ATTITUDE & AVAILABILITY

I love those that thunder out the Word.
The Christian world is in a dead sleep.
Nothing but a loud voice can awake them out of it.

Jonathan Goforth (IMG, 23)

❖ ❖ ❖

People who do not know the Lord ask why in the
world we waste our lives as missionaries. They forget
that they too are expending their lives ... and when
the bubble has burst, they will have nothing of eternal
significance to show for the years they have wasted.

Nate Saint (SNU)

During the last world war, on the Gold Coast of Africa, there lived an elderly African man who had honorably served his Majesty's government and had been given a small pension. With it he retired to the hills to farm. One day while he was working with his hoe, he heard a message come by drumbeat across the jungle forest. He stopped to listen and to translate it for himself. He learned that a great war had begun and that his Majesty's government was in great need of help. About a week later at the little ramshackle post office down on the coast, the postmaster processed a grimy little postcard on which this eloquent message was written, "Your Majesty, I am coming." May God hear that from hundreds of hearts today: "Here am I, send me."

Warren Webster (WW1)

❖   ❖   ❖

I must obey my Master and preach His gospel, regardless of threats or suffering.

Sadhu Sundar Singh (MCC, 32)

Arrogance and self-pity will be the major barriers to pursuing world evangelization. Arrogance with ethno-superiority can be hidden within the justified vision for world evangelization. Self-pity undermines God's work in us and through us. There is a rich heritage of the modern Western Protestant Mission from which the non-Western Christian community can learn. The faith and perseverance of Western missionaries who gave their lives for the sake of the gospel should be rediscovered. The stories should be retold. On the other hand, there is also a spiritual vibrancy from the Global South that the Western world needs to observe.

Patrick Fung (PF1)

AUTHORITY

Do you love the Lord's appearing? Then you will bend every effort to take the gospel into all the world. It troubles me in the light of the clear teaching of God's Word, in the light of our Lord's explicit definition of our task in the Great Commission (Matt 28:18–20) that we take it so lightly. "All authority in heaven and on earth has been given to me." This is the Good News of the Kingdom. Christ has wrested authority from Satan. The Kingdom of God has attacked the kingdom of Satan; this evil Age has been assaulted by The Age to come in the person of Christ. All authority is now His. He will not display this authority in its final glorious victory until He comes again, but the authority is now His. Satan is defeated and bound; death is conquered; sin is broken. All authority is His.

George Eldon Ladd (PWCM, 77)

His authority on earth allows us to dare to go to all the nations. His authority in heaven gives us our only hope of success. And His presence with us leaves us no other choice.

John R. W. Stott (PWCM, 21)

❖ ❖ ❖

Without the Bible world evangelization would be not only impossible but actually inconceivable. It is the Bible that lays upon us the responsibility to evangelize the world, gives us a gospel to proclaim, tells us how to proclaim it, and promises us that it is God's power for salvation to every believer. It is, moreover, an observable fact of history, both past and contemporary, that the degree of the Church's commitment to world evangelization is commensurate with the degree of its conviction about the authority of the Bible. Whenever Christians lose their confidence in the Bible, they also lose their zeal for evangelization. Conversely, whenever they are convinced about the Bible, then they are determined about evangelization.

John R. W. Stott (PWCM, 2)

God's authority over all creation is invested in the Son, Jesus Christ, and it is this Christ who commissions the church to be his witnesses and calls men and women of every people, nation and tongue to submit to his lordship. If we are to take the straightforward teaching of the Bible seriously, we can confidently maintain the validity of God's universal claims upon men and women—indeed, upon all creation. For this reason Christian mission—insofar as it is in harmony with God's own mission—has universal legitimacy. The Great Commission is universal in its scope: "all nations" (Matt 28:19), "to the very end of the age" (Matt 28:20), "all creation" (Mark 16:15), "all nations" (Luke 24:47), "to the ends of the earth" (Acts 1:8).

Craig Ott (ETM, 58–59)

❖ ❖ ❖

The Great Commission is not an option to be considered; it is a command to be obeyed.

J. Hudson Taylor (OMF)

People who don't believe in missions have not read
the New Testament. Right from the beginning Jesus
said the field is the world. The early church took Him
at His word and went East, West, North and South.

———

J. Howard Edington (GMN)

Bible & Missions

Our mandate for world evangelization, therefore, is the whole Bible. It is to be found in the creation of God (because of which all human beings are responsible to him), in the character of God (as outgoing, loving, compassionate, not willing that any should perish, desiring that all should come to repentance), in the promises of God (that all nations will be blessed through Abraham's seed and will become the Messiah's inheritance), the Christ of God (now exalted with universal authority, to receive universal acclaim), in the Spirit of God (who convicts of sin, witnesses to Christ, and impels the church to evangelize) and in the Church of God (which is a multinational, missionary community, under orders to evangelize until Christ returns).

John R. W. Stott (PWCM, 22)

The first words Luke employed in the describing of the church of Pentecost were "they continued steadfastly in the apostles' *doctrine* and fellowship" (Acts 2:42). The last admonition of Paul to Timothy was that he be "a good minister of Jesus Christ, nourished in the words of faith and of *good doctrine*" (I Tim 4:6). The apostles' doctrine—good doctrine—is unchangeable but it is not static. It must be encoded in words, but it must not be entombed in them.

———

David Hesselgrave (DH1, 9)

❖ ❖ ❖

The greatest missionary is the Bible in the mother tongue. It never needs a furlough, is never considered a foreigner.

———

William Cameron Townsend (STV, 110)

❖ ❖ ❖

If you take missions out of the Bible, you won't have anything left but the covers.

———

Nina Gunter (SNU)

I believe twenty-first century missiology will have to wrestle with the doctrine of Scripture that moves beyond the way Evangelical scholarship has tended to defend the inspiration and authority of the Bible with the concepts and methods of modernity itself ... since there is no mission without the authority of Christ himself, and our access to that authority depends upon the Scriptures. So a major missiological task for Evangelical theology will be a fresh articulation of the authority of the Bible and its relation to Christ's authorization of our mission.

Christopher J. H. Wright (GMC, 76)

❖ ❖ ❖

If the Great Commission is true, our plans are not too big; they are too small.

Pat Morley (SNU)

❖ ❖ ❖

The Bible is not the basis of missions; missions is the basis of the Bible.

Ralph Winter (SNU)

What we may conclude from the wording of Genesis 12:3 and its use in the New Testament is that God's purpose for the world is that the blessing of Abraham, namely, the salvation achieved through Jesus Christ, the seed of Abraham, would reach to all the ethnic people groups of the world. This would happen as people in each group put their faith in Christ and thus become "sons of Abraham" (Gal 3:7) and heirs of the promise (Gal 3:29). This event of individual salvation as persons trust Christ will happen among "all the nations."

John Piper (PWCM, 115)

❖ ❖ ❖

The Bible itself is missionary literature from beginning to end. In Genesis we read of the God who made all things. In Revelation we read of the consummation, when all things are made new. And in between we read of the divine concern for the redemption of a world of sinful men. Since the Bible is itself a missionary textbook, we should not expect to find either the basis or the motivation for missions in a single verse of scripture, but, rather, in the tenor and teaching of the Bible as a whole.

Warren Webster (WW1)

When I left England, my hope of India's conversion
was very strong; but amongst so many obstacles, it
would die, unless upheld by God. Well, I have God,
and His Word is true. Though the superstitions
of the heathen were a thousand times stronger
than they are, and the example of the Europeans a
thousand times worse; though I were deserted by
all and persecuted by all, yet my faith, fixed on the
sure Word, would rise above all obstructions and
overcome every trial. God's cause will triumph.

William Carey (TPH, 140)

❖ ❖ ❖

The Bible is from start to finish a missionary book,
for it is the story of God himself reaching into human
history to reconcile a fallen and rebellious humanity to
himself and to reestablish his reign over all creation.
In this sense God is a missionary God—a God who
sends his emissaries, messengers, and ultimately his
Son as agents in this story of salvation. This salvation
will ultimately reach out to include persons of
every people, nation, tribe, and tongue. It is God's
initiative, and it is God who receives all glory.

Craig Ott (ETM, 3)

Submission to Scripture is fundamental to everyday Christian living, for without it Christian discipleship, Christian integrity, Christian freedom and Christian witness are all seriously damaged if not actually destroyed.

John R. W. Stott (JS1)

CALLING

The call of Jesus is personal but not purely individual; Jesus summons his followers not only to an individual calling but also to a corporate calling. … We are not summoned to be a bunch of individual believers, rather to be a community of faith. In the New Testament, it is not so much that there are different churches in different places as that there is one church in many places.

Os Guinness (OG, 98 & 101)

❖ ❖ ❖

If in the sight of God you cannot say you are sure that you have a special call to stay at home, why are you disobeying the Savior's plain command to go?

J. Hudson Taylor (TET)

God has called enough men and women to evangelize all the yet unreached tribes of the earth. Why do I believe that? Because everywhere I go, I constantly meet with men and women who say to me, "When I was young I wanted to be a missionary, but I got married instead," or, "My parents dissuaded me," or some such thing. No it is not God who does not call. It is man who will not respond.

Isobel Kuhn (BSWE)

❖ ❖ ❖

To know the will of God we need an open Bible and an open map.

William Carey (SNU)

❖ ❖ ❖

What higher commission could a human being have than to be Christ's ambassador, His personal representative? Amazingly enough, that is the very mission to which each one of us as a Christian has been called: to be an ambassador for Christ. We are all on an awesome assignment in this life.

John Woodbridge (AFC, 10–11)

If there is no Caller, there are no callings—only work.
… We are not primarily called to do something or go
somewhere; we are called to Someone.

Os Guinness (OG, 42–43)

The one aim of the call of God is the satisfaction of
God, not a call to do something for Him.

Oswald Chambers (MUFH2)

I hope, dear father, you may be enabled to surrender
me up to the Lord for the most arduous, honorable,
and important work that ever any of the sons of
men were called to engage in. I have many sacrifices
to make. I must part with a beloved family, and a
number of most affectionate friends. Never did I see
such sorrow manifested as reigned through our place
of worship last Lord's day. But I have set my hand to
the plough.

William Carey, shortly before sailing for India (MWC, 64)

CALLING

The missionary call includes an awareness of the
needs of a lost world, the commands of Christ,
a concern for the lost, a radical commitment to
God, your church's affirmation, blessing and
commissioning, a passionate desire, the Spirit's
gifting, and an indescribable yearning that motivates
beyond all understanding.

David Sills (TMC, 30)

❖ ❖ ❖

When God's finger points, God's hand will open
the door.

Clarence W. Jones, Founder HCJB Global (CUTM, 65)

❖ ❖ ❖

The missionary call is a personal challenge by God
to engage in fulfilling the Great Commission in the
spirit of the Great Commandment, with the focus of
the Great Compassion.

David Sills (TMC)

17

The question for us to answer is not, "Am I called to the foreign field?" but, "Can I show sufficient cause for not going?"

Robert E. Speer (TET)

❖ ❖ ❖

When God calls His child to live the life of a missionary, He gives him the desire with the calling.

David Sills (TMC)

❖ ❖ ❖

I wasn't God's first choice for what I've done for China. ... I don't know who was. ... It must have been a man ... a well-educated man. I don't know what happened. Perhaps he died. Perhaps he wasn't willing. ... And God looked down ... and saw Gladys Aylward ... and God said—"Well she's willing!"

Gladys Aylward (BSWE)

❖ ❖ ❖

Hearing the missionary call has a great deal to do with what you are listening for.

David Sills (TMC, 202)

Had I cared for the comments of people, I should never have been a missionary.

C. T. Studd (BSWE)

❖ ❖ ❖

God's call is indeed a mystery. So is God's hand of power at work in our world. One thing is certain, only those willing to hear and follow His call by faith through the open door before them will experience the amazement of walking with God into the unknown. Only those who take the call will personally know His power, and presence, which comes along with His call. His voice is not always a dramatic peal of thunder from the clouds. Sometimes it is a still, small voice.

Michael Loftis (ML1)

❖ ❖ ❖

A man not spiritually fitted ought not to go, but neither is he fit to stay.

Robert E. Speer (TET)

God's call doesn't register in a vacuum; only a person who is committed to doing God's will can receive a call.

Thomas Hale (OBM, 18)

❖   ❖   ❖

In the biblical understanding of giftedness, gifts are never really ours or for ourselves. Our gifts are ultimately God's, and we are only "stewards." ... The truth is not that God is finding us a place for our gifts but that God has created us and our gifts for a place of his choosing.

Os Guinness (OG, 47)

❖   ❖   ❖

There are two very simple biblical truths that relate to world missions: the world must hear the gospel and Christ has charged us to take it to them. Why then have the nations not yet heard the gospel after two thousand years? It is not because God has not provided sufficient numbers of Christians, or called sufficient numbers into missions. God calls many more than actually go.

David Sills (TMC, chapter 9)

As long as I see anything to be done for God, life is worth living; but O how vain and unworthy it is to live for any lower end!

David Brainerd (SQB, 141)

❖ ❖ ❖

If you are going to be used by God, He will take you through a number of experiences that are not meant for you personally at all. They are designed to make you useful in His hands, and to enable you to understand what takes place in the lives of others. Because of this process, you will never be surprised by what comes your way. You say, "Oh, I can't deal with that person." Why can't you? God gave you sufficient opportunities to learn from Him about that problem; but you turned away, not heeding the lesson, because it seemed foolish to spend your time that way.

Oswald Chambers (OC, Nov. 5 entry)

❖ ❖ ❖

He is no fool who gives what he cannot keep to gain what he cannot lose.

Jim Elliot, missionary martyr in Ecuador (JEJ)

This is the decision we do not make, because it has already been made. Whether we spend our lives for the purpose of reaching all men with the gospel is not optional. Christ has commanded every Christian to do just this. Now there are many different ways of accomplishing this one purpose—but regardless of the particular work God has for each of us to do, the one aim of us all in doing our particular job for the Lord must be the evangelization of the whole world.

G. Allen Fleece (WGD, 64)

❖ ❖ ❖

If God has called you to China or any other place and you are sure in your own heart, let nothing deter you ... remember it is God who has called you and it is the same as when He called Moses or Samuel.

Gladys Aylward (TGE, 126)

❖ ❖ ❖

If a commission by an earthly king is considered a[n] honor, how can a commission by a Heavenly King be considered a sacrifice?

David Livingstone (SNU)

I thought of all God's people looking out after me with expectation, following me with their wishes and prayers. I thought of the holy angels, some of whom perhaps were guarding me on my way; and of God and Christ approving my course and mission. Who will go for me? Here am I, send me.

Henry Martyn (MHM, 122)

❖   ❖   ❖

The term "missionary call" should never have been coined. It is not Scriptural and therefore can be harmful. Thousands of youth desiring to serve the Lord have waited and waited for some mysterious "missionary call" that never came. After a time they became weary in waiting and gave up the idea of going to the mission field. Does this mean that there is no such thing as a call of any kind? No, indeed. There is a call, a very definite call, to the service of God on a full-time basis. Jesus "called" Peter and Andrew to follow Him. "Immediately they left their nets and followed him" (Matt 4:20). Later He "called" James and John. "Immediately they left the boat and their father, and followed him" (Matt 4:22).

J. Herbert Kane (UCM, 41)

Let us remind ourselves that the Great Commission was never qualified by clauses calling for advance only if funds were plentiful and no hardship or self-denial involved. On the contrary, we are told to expect tribulation and even persecution, but with it victory in Christ. ... It is ours to show, in the salvation of our Lord Jesus Christ, and in personal communion with him, a joy unspeakable and full of glory that cannot be affected by outside circumstances.

John Stam (JSGA)

❖   ❖   ❖

If God calls you to be a missionary,
don't stoop to be a king.

Jordan Grooms (SNU)

❖   ❖   ❖

To preach the Gospel requires that the preacher should believe that he is sent to those whom he is addressing at the moment, because God has among them those whom He is at the moment calling; it requires that the speaker should expect a response.

Roland Allen (MM, 74)

But ultimately only one thing can conquer choice—being chosen. Thus, for followers of Christ, calling neutralizes the fundamental poison of choice in modern life. "I have chosen you," Jesus said, "you have not chosen me." We are not our own; we have been bought with a price. We have no rights, only responsibilities. Following Christ is not our initiative, merely our response, in obedience. Once we have been called, we literally "have no choice."

Os Guinness (OG, 177)

❖   ❖   ❖

It is not necessary that we go to the Scriptures, or to the ends of the earth, to discover our obligation to the unevangelized. A knowledge of our own hearts should be sufficient to make plain our duty. We know our need of Christ. How unreasonable, therefore, for us to assume that the nations living in sin and wretchedness and bondage can do without Him whom we so much need even in the most favored Christian lands.

John R. Mott (STV, 69)

How then does one determine whether or not God has in mind some form of missionary vocation? The inner response of a person's spirit to the revelation of God's program in the world and its present state should catapult every true disciple into total involvement in that enterprise. As he becomes involved and presses forward, filling those roles which are open to him and seeking to invest his time and energy in that which will count most for God's kingdom, it is quite appropriate for him to "desire earnestly" the high calling of missionary or even of pioneer missionary evangelist. When multitudes of those who profess faith in Christ become this kind of actively obedient disciple, God will thrust out into the harvest field those laborers whom He has chosen.

Robertson McQuilkin (TGO, 77–78)

✦ ✦ ✦

It is odd that a million Baptists of the South can furnish only three men for all China. Odd that with five hundred preachers in the state of Virginia, we must rely on a Presbyterian to fill a Baptist pulpit (here). I wonder how these things look in heaven. They certainly look very queer in China.

Lottie Moon (GGC, 42)

CHARACTER

The greatest hindrance to the advance of the gospel worldwide is the failure of the lives of God's people.

John R. W. Stott (CTC, 77)

❖ ❖ ❖

In a number of ways, Christianity seems to be losing credibility. Our lifestyles do not support the things we say, our relationships with others, or the way we handle money. Many of these issues discredit us. If we do not have integrity, we are just a bunch of vuvuzella blowers who are blowing but not actively playing on the field.

Calisto Odede of Kenya (CO)

Our gospel is cancelled by the way we live.

Henry Blackaby (HB)

❖ ❖ ❖

In encouraging other young men to come out as missionaries, do use a word of caution. One wrong-headed, conscientiously-obstinate fellow would ruin us. Humble, quiet, persevering men; men of sound, sterling talents (though, perhaps, not brilliant), of decent accomplishments, and some natural aptitude to acquire a language; men of an amiable temper, willing to take the lowest place, to be the least of all and the servants of all; men who enjoy closet religion, who live near to God, and are willing to suffer all things for Christ's sake, without being proud of it, these are the men. But O, how unlike to this description is the writer of it.

Adoniram Judson (MLLAJ, 185)

❖ ❖ ❖

The reason some folks don't believe in missions is that the brand of religion they have isn't worth propagating.

Unknown (RFM)

Before we go out to do what God has called us to do, we must first be the people he has created us to be. Before strategy, activity, and analysis comes character. Any serious church planter (or lay Christian, for that matter) must be serious about displaying the fruit of the Spirit and having a Christ-like attitude in all areas of life.

Unknown (EGK, 17)

❖ ❖ ❖

There is no biblical mission without biblical living.

Christopher J. H. Wright (CTC)

❖ ❖ ❖

Our witness becomes dramatically more attractive and credible to nondisciples as they see us expressing unusual grace in the face of the crushing circumstances that often bring out the worst in people. If we can display a truly Christ-like character when we are under pressure, it will create curiosity and conversation about our faith and values.

Daniel Meyer (WE, 157)

When we say that the missionary fills a unique
role we do not imply that he is better than others,
simply that he is different. He is not necessarily
more spiritual than the pastor, or even the layman,
who remains at home. Nor will his reward at the
judgment seat of Christ be any greater. He is
the servant of Christ and will be asked the same
questions and judged on the same basis as anyone
else. Did he seek to promote his own glory or
was he concerned solely for the glory of God (I
Cor 10:31)? Was he motivated by some personal
considerations or was he constrained by the love
of Christ (I Cor 13:1–3)? Did he do his work
in the energy of the flesh or in the power of
the Holy Spirit (Acts 1:8)? If he can answer all
three questions correctly he will have his reward;
otherwise his work will be judged to be wood, hay,
and stubble to be consumed in the fire (I Cor 3:12–
15). The missionary is not better than his fellow
workers, just different.

J. Herbert Kane (UCM, 30)

Strengthening our credibility with others requires an honest awareness and open confession of our own untransformed character and a purposeful commitment to seeking the help of God and others in repairing these sins. As people see us clearly naming and sincerely crucifying the sins that limit our lives, they will become more interested in pursuing this pathway to authentic life-change for themselves.

Daniel Meyer (WE, 141)

Church & Missions

God is a missionary God. The Bible is a missionary book. The gospel is a missionary message. The church is a missionary institution. And when the church ceases to be missionary minded, it has denied its faith and betrayed its trust.

J. Herbert Kane (TMOM, 1)

✦ ✦ ✦

The Church is by nature missionary to the extent that, if it ceases to be missionary, it has not just failed in one of its tasks, it has ceased to be the Church. Thus, the Church's self-understanding and sense of identity (its ecclesiology) is inherently bound up with its call to share and live out the Gospel of Jesus Christ to the ends of the earth and the end of time.

Andrew Kirk (WIM, 30–31)

It is one thing for a minister to be an advocate and supporter of missions: it is another and very different thing for him to understand that missions are the chief end of the Church, and therefore the chief end for which his congregation exists. ... He must learn how to lead the congregation on to make the extension of Christ's kingdom the highest object of its corporate existence.

Andrew Murray (AM, 15)

❖ ❖ ❖

In the long run the spiritual tone of the missionaries and the mission congregation abroad cannot be higher than that of the home church out of which it was born. Great advances in missions are always connected with a deep revival of spiritual life, and a higher devotion to the Lord Jesus.

Andrew Murray (AM, 55)

❖ ❖ ❖

The best remedy for a sick church is to put it on a missionary diet.

Unknown (HM)

If one wants to maintain a specifically theological meaning of the term "mission" as "foreign mission(s)," its significance is, in my opinion, that it keeps calling the Church to think of its essential nature as a community sent forth into the world. Seen in that light missionary work is not just one of its activities, but the criterion for all its activities. Missionary work reflects in a unique way, particularly in its passing boundaries in space and spirit, the very essence of the Church as a Church. It returns, as it were, to its origin, and is confronted with its missionary calling. It is exactly by going outside itself that the Church is itself and comes to itself.

Craig Ott (ETM, xiv)

❖ ❖ ❖

Napoleon once said, "It is a maxim in the military art that the army which remains in its entrenchment is beaten." The non-missionary Church sins against its own best interest and is inviting defeat. A stay-at-home Christianity is not real Christianity at all.

J. Ross Stevenson (JRS)

The intimate connection between Christ's life and
work and the Great Commission makes inescapable
the conclusion that the missionary mandate is not
simply one among many good things that the church
should do. It is more than just another "program." It
is the integration point of the church's entire calling.
Nor can any good work be considered mission,
irrespective of its relationship to Christ's work.

Craig Ott (ETM, 41)

❖ ❖ ❖

It is just as proper, maybe even more so, to say
Christ's global cause has a Church as to say Christ's
Church has a global cause.

David Bryant (TTT)

❖ ❖ ❖

Mission work does not arise from any arrogance in
the Christian Church: mission is its cause and its life.
The Church exists by mission, just as fire exists by
burning.

Emil Brunner (WS, 124)

I spent twenty years of my life trying to recruit people out of local churches and into missions structures so that they could be involved in fulfilling God's global mission. Now I have another idea. Let's take God's global mission and put it right in the middle of the local church!

George Miley (TTT)

❖   ❖   ❖

The church remains God's primary agent to accomplish his purposes in this age. The planting and growth of Christ-centered, Bible-believing, Spirit-filled churches is God's chosen way to multiply a witness to his kingdom on earth. God has surely used individuals, even godless kings and potentates to accomplish his purposes. But the church remains the only community that is uniquely called to live out the values of the kingdom (1 Pet 2:9).

Craig Ott (ETM, 119)

❖   ❖   ❖

The mission of the church is missions; the mission of missions is the church.

Lesslie Newbigin (MJN, 105)

Mission … is seen as a movement from God to the world; the Church is viewed as an instrument for that mission. There is a church because there is mission, not vice versa.

David J. Bosch (TM)

❖ ❖ ❖

An introverted church, turned in on itself, preoccupied with its own survival, has virtually forfeited the right to be a church, for it is denying a major part of its own being. As a planet which ceases to be in orbit is no longer a planet, so a church which ceases to be in mission is no longer a church.

John R. W. Stott (JS2)

❖ ❖ ❖

If the church is central to God's purpose, as seen in both history and the gospel, it must surely also be central to our lives. How can we take lightly what God takes so seriously? How dare we push to the circumference what God has placed at the centre?

John R. W. Stott (WSG, 105)

The church is the pilgrim people of God. It is
on the move—hastening to the ends of the earth
to beseech all men to be reconciled to God, and
hastening to the end of time to meet its Lord who
will gather all into one.

Lesslie Newbigin (LN1, 25)

A Church which has ceased to be a mission has
lost the essential character of a Church. ... An
unchurchly mission is as much of a monstrosity as
an unmissionary Church. ... No recovery of the true
wholeness of the Church's nature is possible without
a recovery of its radically missionary character.

Lesslie Newbigin (LN1, 169)

Responsible churches are made up of responsible
members. This principle is vital to effective
evangelism. Accepting Christ as Savior means
accepting him as Lord. And this means responsible
church-relatedness.

Vergil Gerber (EGK, 61)

If the Church is "in Christ," she is involved in mission. Her whole existence then has a missionary character. Her conduct as well as her words will convince the unbelievers and put their ignorance and stupidity to silence.

David J. Bosch (HM)

❖   ❖   ❖

The New Testament knows little of an individualized faith separated from Christian community. If we speak of evangelism, we must also speak of the church. In the book of Acts, we see God himself "adding" new believers to the church (Acts 2:41,47; 5:14). One cannot read Acts without noting that nearly everywhere the gospel was preached, communities of believers are formed. Evangelism led to the establishment of churches under a local spiritual leadership and interrelated with other churches. To belong to Christ is also to belong to Christ's people (1 Cor 12:13).

Craig Ott (ETM, 118)

There is widespread awareness that the energy and capacity of the missions movement would be enhanced if we could bring more local churches into meaningful participation. The vast majority of all resources God has entrusted to His people—He has placed in local churches.

George Miley (LTC, 66)

❖ ❖ ❖

It is critically important—especially in a worldwide, multicultural situation such as the Church faces today—to be clear that the essence of the Church is people, not organization: that it is a community, not an institution. The great divide in contemporary thinking about the Church is located precisely here. Biblically, the Church is the community of God's people, and this is a spiritual reality which is valid in every culture. But all ecclesiastical institutions— whether seminaries, denominational structures, mission boards, publishing houses or what have you—are not the Church. Rather, they are supportive institutions created to serve the Church in its life and mission.

Howard A. Snyder (PWCM, 140)

The Church must send or the church will end.

Mendell Taylor (SNU)

❖ ❖ ❖

The local church is the cradle of missions. It is the place where mission vision is rooted ... the place where mission passion is incubated ... the place where concern for the lost is highlighted ... the place where mission agencies discover their greatest asset—missionaries! The church is the place from where missionaries are commended for service ... the place where mission funding is generated ... the place where corporate prayers for missionaries are offered ... the place where furloughed missionaries report, rest, get replenished and renewed ... the place from where returned missionaries spring forth to cross cultures once again to bring people into the fullness of Christ. Local churches are both the anchor and the lifeline of missions.

M. Newell (V1, 1)

There is nothing in the world or the Church—
except the church's disobedience—to render the
evangelization of the world in this generation an
impossibility.

Robert E. Speer (GMN)

❖   ❖   ❖

A congregation that is not deeply and earnestly
involved in the worldwide proclamation of the gospel
does not understand the nature of salvation.

Ted Engstrom (SNU)

❖   ❖   ❖

The mark of a great church is not its seating capacity,
but its sending capacity.

Mike Stachura (SNU)

❖   ❖   ❖

The average pastor views his church as a local church
with a missions program; while he ought to realize
that if he is in fact pastoring a church, it is to be a
global church with a missions purpose.

Unknown (SNU)

The scriptures tell us of no other people, no other message, no other power, no other movement that is the instrument of God's choosing for fulfilling his purposes in this age as is the church.

Craig Ott (ETM, 196)

❖ ❖ ❖

It is not the church's responsibility to right every wrong or to meet every need, though we have biblical motivation to do some or both. It is our responsibility, however—our unique mission and plain priority—that this unpopular, impractical gospel message gets told, that neighbors and nations may know that Jesus is the Christ, the Son of God, and that by believing, they may have life in his name.

Kevin Deyoung and Greg Gilbert (WMC, 249)

CHURCH PLANTING

Missions exists to plant Christ-purchased, God-exalting, worshipping communities of the redeemed in all the peoples of the world. The passion of a missionary—as distinct from that of an evangelist—is to plant a worshipping community of Christians in a people group who has no access to the gospel because of language or cultural barriers.

Craig Ott (ETM, 118)

❖ ❖ ❖

We'd be wrong to send out planters with organizational, strategic, and marketing tools but not the fundamental truths of God's Word and the principles of Scripture from which to work.

Ed Stetzer (PMC, 37)

You might say, "I'm not called to plant churches." Yes, you are! It's always the will of God to have a people who worship His Son in the nations. You'll never have to worry about making God mad if you try to plant a church. It seems crazy to me that people are under the delusion they need a special calling to save souls, to disciple them, and to get them together to love Jesus. Whatever ministry you are with, you must understand one thing: church planting is not for us, it's for God. We do it so God will have a people to worship Him!

Floyd McClung (PWCM, 186)

❖ ❖ ❖

The planting, establishing, and growth of churches are central to the flow of salvation history and the expressed will of Jesus Christ. Throughout salvation history God has chosen to work through a people. In the Old Testament that people was primarily Israel, and in the New it is the church. Church planting and growth are Christ's own work, for he has said, "I will build my church" (Matt 16:18b). Jesus's work of redemption was not merely to save individuals, but he "gave himself for us to redeem us from all wickedness and to purify for himself a people that are his very own, eager to do what is good" (Titus 2:14).

Craig Ott (ETM, 118)

Church planting should not be understood merely pragmatically as an effective means of evangelism. The church is the bride of Christ. He gave himself for her and is sanctifying her to present her to himself in all purity, beauty, and glory (Eph 5:25–27). Thus, to plant and build up the church in love and holiness is to beautify the bride of Christ.

Craig Ott (ETM, 119)

❖ ❖ ❖

Where there are no churches, there shall be churches. The Apostle Paul captured this central thrust of biblical missions when he testified to the Christians living in Rome: "And I have so made it my aim to preach the gospel, not where Christ was named, lest I should build on another man's foundation" (Rom 15:20). Cultural boundaries must be crossed. Social barriers must be penetrated. Linguistic obstacles must be bridged. Religious resistance must be overcome. A church movement must be brought into being within each people group. Churches that feel a responsibility themselves to work cross-culturally must be planted. That is the purpose of missions.

Kenneth B. Mulholland (PWCM, 136)

But in many ways the selection and training of leaders are the most important aspects of church planting because these individuals will not only manage church affairs, they will model the faith for good or ill.

David J. Hesselgrave (DH2, 276)

❖ ❖ ❖

Missionary efforts that do not in some way work toward planting and nurturing churches are fundamentally flawed. Simply put, the establishing and nurturing of churches is core to our call as followers of Christ. While this goal is constant, the circumstances in which it happens and means by which it is accomplished is ever shifting, and we always need fresh reminders of age-old lessons to maintain our focus.

Scott Moreau (EMQ2, "A Word from the Editor")

❖ ❖ ❖

Church planting is not an end in itself, but one aspect of the mission of God in which churches are privileged to participate.

Stuart Murray (SM, 30)

The essential missionary task is to establish a viable indigenous church planting movement that carries the potential to renew whole extended families and transform whole societies. It is viable in that it can grow on its own, indigenous meaning that it is not seen as foreign, and a church planting movement that continues to reproduce intergenerational fellowships that are able to evangelize the rest of the people group.

Winter and Koch (BAM, 125)

❖ ❖ ❖

Whenever the demands of the ministry detract from the church planter's devotional times, an ethical dilemma exists. Missionaries cannot substitute time spent on building the church for spending time with the one who promised to build His Church.

J. D. Payne (EMQ1, 94)

COMMITMENT

God had an only son and he was a missionary.
A poor, poor example of him I am. But in this work
I now live. And in this work, I wish to die.

David Livingstone (TET)

❖ ❖ ❖

When I go to the cross … and enter into His passion,
then my passion is revived and my vision is renewed.
… Our calling as evangelists is not to silver or satin or
silk or stones precious, but to blood, toil, tears, and
sweat. May our commitment be so complete that we
will make hell gasp for breath. Yes, our commitment
needs to be that complete.

George Sweeting (MBI, 90)

Life is short. Happiness consists not in outward circumstances. Millions of Burmans are perishing. I am almost the only person on earth who has attained their language to such a degree as to be able to communicate the way of salvation. How great are my obligations to spend and be spent for Christ! What a privilege to be allowed to serve him ... and suffer for him. ... But in myself I am absolute nothingness. ... Soon we shall be in heaven. Oh, let us live as we shall then wish we had done!

Adoniram Judson (RHH, 90)

❖ ❖ ❖

We who have Christ's eternal life need to throw away our own lives.

George Verwer (BSWE)

❖ ❖ ❖

The motto of every missionary, whether preacher, printer, or schoolmaster, ought to be "Devoted for life."

Adoniram Judson (TGS, 409)

COMMITMENT

My soul longs to feel more of a pilgrim and stranger here below, that nothing may divert me from pressing through the lonely desert, till I arrive at my Father's house.

David Brainerd (LDB, 40)

❖ ❖ ❖

The way I see it, we ought to be willing to die. In the military, we were taught that to obtain our objectives we had to be willing to be expendable. Missionaries must face that same expendability.

Nate Saint (UV, 17)

COMPASSION
(LOVE)

Love is the root of missions; sacrifice is the fruit of missions.

Roderick Davis (SNU)

❖ ❖ ❖

Mission has its origin in the heart of God. God is a fountain of sending love. This is the deepest source of mission. It is impossible to penetrate deeper still; there is mission because God loves people.

David J. Bosch (ETM, 61)

❖ ❖ ❖

True love is always costly.

Billy Graham (TGC, 152)

Dear Jesus,

Today I read in Your Word about loving our enemies.
God, we have so many enemies these days. ...
In Romans 12 You tell us not to repay anyone evil for
evil, but rather to be careful to do what is right in the
eyes of everybody. To live at peace with all men.

Bonnie Witherall

❖ ❖ ❖

Each person out there, whether young or old,
anorexic or obese, short or tall, beautiful or ugly,
black or white, straight or gay, tattooed or not, is
a person created by God, whom God loves with
abandon, and for whom God died. Our job is to
extend that kind of love to them. We must never
allow ourselves to think that they are an object
for our success. The measurements that we in the
evangelical community often use, "souls saved, church
membership, youth group attendees," are poison ...
and demeaning to anyone else. Jesus looked at the
rich young ruler and "loved him." He didn't see
him as an object or number, he saw him as a
complete person.

Charles Davis (CD2)

Missionaries have always been apostles of love. Count Zinzendorf, the greatest missionary statesman of the eighteenth century, said: "I have one passion, it is He and He alone." Hudson Taylor, who gave fifty years to the service of Christ in China, said: "If I had a thousand lives, I'd give them all to China." Alexander Mackay, writing to the Church Missionary Society, said: "My heart burns for the deliverance of Africa." Melville Cox died after being in Liberia only four months. His last words were: "Let a thousand fall before Africa be given up." Henry Martyn on his arrival in India said, "Now let me burn out for God." All these men were, like Paul, constrained by the love of Christ (2 Cor 5:14) and they literally burned themselves out for God and man.

J. Herbert Kane (UCM, 34)

❖ ❖ ❖

Jesus says to us that when we give a cup of water to "the least of these" we do it unto Him. Every time someone at the clinic asks me for a cup of water I give it to them, knowing I'm giving it to someone Jesus loves and cares for.

Bonnie Witherall, missionary martyr in Lebanon (AMG, 23)

Let my heart be broken with the things that break God's heart.

Bob Pierce, World Vision (GMN)

❖ ❖ ❖

Compassion costs. It is easy enough to argue, criticize and condemn, but redemption is costly, and comfort draws from the deep. Brains can argue, but it takes heart to comfort.

Samuel Chadwick (CQR)

❖ ❖ ❖

If the love in our hearts is Christ's love, we shall not shrink from sacrificial service, from a service which is costly in energy, dignity, money or time.

John R. W. Stott (JS)

❖ ❖ ❖

Be warm and merciful and let no one go from you empty-handed. The least you can offer is your time and patience, your affection and your prayer.

Unknown (DCQ)

To wipe all tears from off all faces is a task too hard for mortals; but to alleviate misfortunes is often within the most limited power: yet the opportunities which every day affords of relieving the most wretched of human beings are overlooked and neglected with equal disregard of policy and goodness.

Samuel Johnson (SJ)

❖ ❖ ❖

Missionary zeal does not grow out of intellectual beliefs, nor out of theological arguments, but out of love. If I do not love a person I am not moved to help him by proofs that he is in need; if I do love him, I wait for no proof of a special need to urge me to help him.

Roland Allen (RAQ)

❖ ❖ ❖

My understanding leaves me, my memory fails me, my utterance fails me, but *I thank God, my charity holds out still.* I find *that* rather grows than fails.

John Eliot (GM, 29)

CONTEXTUALIZATION

Inasmuch as all native churches grow up into
the fullness of the stature of Christ, distinctions
and defects will vanish. ... But it may be doubted
whether, to the last, the Church of Christ will not
exhibit marked national characteristics which, in the
overruling grace of God, will tend to its perfection
and glory.

——————

Henry Venn (HV, 284)

❖ ❖ ❖

Let us in everything unsinful become Chinese, that
by all means we may save some. Let us adopt their
costume, acquire their language, study to imitate
their habits ... live in their houses.

——————

J. Hudson Taylor (TGC, 180)

Why should a foreign aspect be given to Christianity?
We wish to see churches of such believers presided
over by pastors and officers of their own countrymen,
worshipping God in their own tongue, in edifices of
a thoroughly native style.

J. Hudson Taylor (HT, Chapter 6)

❖ ❖ ❖

The key tension of contextualization is the
relationship between the universal absolutes of
Scripture and the peculiarities of cultural differences.
But the tension can be creative and fruitful. An
overemphasis on the absolutes leads to irreverent
application, while an overemphasis on culture can
lead to relativistic absurdity.

James Plueddemann (LAC, 150)

❖ ❖ ❖

The Indian is making an amazing discovery, namely
that Christianity and Jesus are not the same—that they
may have Jesus without the system that has been built
up around Him in the West.

E. Stanley Jones (TTT)

CONTEXTUALIZATION

That Word is to pass into all those distinctive ways of
thought, those networks of kinship, those special ways
of doing things, that give the nation its commonality,
its coherence, its identity. It has to travel through the
shared mental and moral processes of community,
the way that decisions are made in that community.
Christ is to become actualized—to become flesh,
as it were—as distinctively, and may I say it, as
appropriately—as when he lived as a Palestinian Jew in
the early first century.

———

Andrew F. Walls (TGC, 180)

CULTURE

Christianity affects cultures by moving them to a position short of the absolute, and it does this by placing God at the centre. The point of departure for the church in mission ... is Pentecost, with Christianity triumphing by relinquishing Jerusalem or any fixed universal centre, be it geographical, linguistic or cultural, and with the result of there being a proliferation of centres, languages and cultures within the church. Christian ecumenism is the pluralism of the periphery with only God at the centre. Consequently all cultural expressions remain at the periphery of truth, all equal in terms of access, but all equally inadequate in terms of what is ultimate and final.

Lamin Sanneh (GLC, 61)

To disturb and to destroy the religious beliefs, rites, and ceremonies of any people is to make an attack on the sanctuary of the soul, which can only be excused if he who delivers it has the certainty that what he offers is indeed the pearl of great price, to obtain which the surrender of the most sacred possessions cannot be regarded as too high a sacrifice.

A. E. Garvie (WC)

❖ ❖ ❖

The missionary ... is the bearer of culture. He has not only an evangelistic mandate; he has a cultural mandate as well. He is his brother's keeper. The good things of life that he enjoys are not really his. They are God's gifts to mankind. It so happens that they occur in greater abundance in the Western world. This does not give us the right to keep them to ourselves. As followers of Jesus Christ we are duty bound to love our neighbors as ourselves (Matt 22:39), and we must love them in deed and in truth, not simply in word or speech (1 John 3:18).

J. Herbert Kane (UCM)

Jesus within Jewish culture, Paul within Hellenistic culture, take it for granted that there will be rubs and frictions—not from the adoption of a new culture, but from the transformation of the mind toward that of Christ.

Andrew F. Walls (AW, 8)

❖   ❖   ❖

The more we interact with each other, the more we need to understand each other's underlying cultural values. The more churches in the West and Asia partner with churches in Africa and Latin America, the more deeply we need to be aware of how culture permeates hidden assumptions about leadership. External similarities in global leadership can lull us into complacency. We may think we understand leaders in other cultures when in fact our ignorance can cause serious misunderstandings. Globalization means that people are looking more and more alike on the outside, but the inner layer of cultural values hasn't changed very much.

James Plueddemann (LAC, 73–74)

The fact, then, that "If any man is in Christ he is a new creation" does not mean that he starts or continues his life in a vacuum, or that his mind is a blank table. It has been formed by his own culture and history, and since God has accepted him as he is, his Christian mind will continue to be influenced by what was in it before. And this is as true for groups as for persons. All churches are culture churches—including our own.

Andrew F. Walls (AW, 8)

❖ ❖ ❖

Not only does God take people as they are: He takes them in order to transform them into what He wants them to be. Along with the indigenizing principle which makes his faith a place to feel at home, the Christian inherits the pilgrim principle, which whispers to him that he has no abiding city and warns him that to be faithful to Christ will put him out of step with his society; for that society never existed, in East or West, ancient time or modern, which could absorb the word of Christ painlessly into its system.

Andrew F. Walls (AW, 8)

The gospel is always understood and lived out with a culture, but it stands apart from and is distinguished from all cultures. It can be comprehended and applied from within every culture. But because all cultures are human, they are all corrupted by sin. So the gospel must also challenge every culture to change and more deeply conform to the will of God.

Stephen Strauss (ETM, 268)

❖ ❖ ❖

Until we are willing for the church to have different manifestations in different cultures—rather than export the denominational patterns rooted in our own history and often irrelevant to the rest of the world—we will not have indigenous churches. It does not matter whether they are "self-governing, self-supporting, and self-propagating" or not. It is not until we are willing to let churches grow also that we have learned to entrust the Holy Spirit with society.

William A. Smalley (PWCM, 479)

Learning a language and culture through
relationships in a community requires a tremendous
commitment to the people of the new language. ...
If your goal is to live with the people, to love and
serve them, and to become a belonger in your new
community, then learning the language will prove
to be a great means to that goal. And learning the
language will probably become quite manageable!

Tom Brewster (CML, 4)

❖ ❖ ❖

If you reject the food, ignore the customs, fear the
religion, and avoid the people, you might better stay
home. You are like a pebble thrown into water; you
become wet on the surface but you are never part of
the water.

James A. Mitchener (JM)

DIFFICULTIES

The unoccupied fields of the world await those who are willing to be lonely for the sake of Christ. To the pioneer missionary, the words of our Lord Jesus Christ to the apostles when He showed them His hands and His feet, come with special force: "As my Father hath sent Me, even so send I you" (John 20:21). He came into the world, and it was a great unoccupied mission field. "He came unto His own, and His own received Him not" (John 1:11). He came and His welcome was derision, His life suffering, and His throne the Cross. As He came, He expects us to go. We must follow in His footprints. The pioneer missionary, in overcoming obstacles and difficulties, has the privilege not only of knowing Christ and the power of His resurrection, but also something of the fellowship of His suffering.

Samuel M. Zwemer (SMZ1, 221)

I have found that there are three stages in every
great work of God: first, it is impossible, then it is
difficult, then it is done.

J. Hudson Taylor (PFI, 5)

❖ ❖ ❖

Difficulties are not without their advantages. They
are not to unnerve us. They are not to be regarded
simply as subjects for discussion nor as grounds for
skepticism and pessimism. They are not to cause
inaction, but rather to intensify activity. They were
made to be overcome. Above all they are to create
profound distrust in human plans and energy, and to
drive us to God.

John R. Mott (SMZ2, 222)

❖ ❖ ❖

The more obstacles you have, the more opportunities
there are for God to do something.

Clarence W. Jones (CWJ)

Many Christians estimate difficulty in the light of their own resources, and thus they attempt very little and they always fail. All giants have been weak men who did great things for God because they reckoned on His power and presence to be with them.

J. Hudson Taylor (DCQ-HT)

❖   ❖   ❖

It (the murder of his son, Elliott) has been so utterly beyond all understanding and so irreparable that there has been nothing to do except to be quiet and to go on steadily doing moment by moment what needed to be done ... and simply trust to infinite wisdom and love.

Robert E. Speer (MSG, 236)

❖   ❖   ❖

The work of a true missionary is work indeed, often very monotonous, apparently not very successful, and carried on through great and varied but unceasing difficulties.

J. Hudson Taylor (ABJ3, 350)

DISAPPOINTMENT
(DISCOURAGEMENT)

Part of the heartache of all missionary work is the bright promising convert who turns out to be a mere puffball, crumbling like a macaroon under the least pressure.

Isobel Kuhn (TET)

❖ ❖ ❖

Could we but see the smallest fruit, we could rejoice midst the privations and toils which we bear; but as it is, our hands do often hang down.

Mary Moffat (TUC, 145)

Sometimes I feel ... that my cross is heavy beyond endurance. ... My heart seems worn out and bruised beyond repair, and in my deep loneliness I often wish to be gone, but God knows best, and I want to do every ounce of work he wants me to do.

———

C. T. Studd (CTS1, 216)

❖ ❖ ❖

Joy and sorrow travel together.

———

Malla Moe (MM, 119)

DISCIPLESHIP
(MAKING DISCIPLES)

Discipleship must always be discipleship-in-movement-to-the-world. The disciple who will not lay down his life for the world and for the gospel of reconciliation is not worthy of being a follower of Jesus Christ.

Charles Van Engen (GMP, 76)

❖ ❖ ❖

The men who followed Him were unique in their generation. They turned the world upside down because their hearts had been turned right side up. The world has never been the same.

Billy Graham (TSH, 8)

Christianity without the living Christ is inevitably
Christianity without discipleship, and Christianity
without discipleship is always Christianity without
Christ.

Dietrich Bonhoeffer (TCOD, 63–64)

❖　❖　❖

Globalization is the process through which human
interconnectedness has reached global proportions.
It is accomplished through information technology
that provides: 1) speed, 2) scope, and 3) synergy. …
Globalization makes evangelism easier, but
discipleship harder.

Os Guinness (OGCT)

❖　❖　❖

The bare minimum that missionaries should teach
must result in trained leadership in the national
church that is able to interpret the Word of God
(2 Tim 2:15), understand basic Christian doctrines
(1 Tim 4:6), and teach them to others (1 Tim 3:2).

David Sills (R&T, 64)

We dare not go on awakening interest in the
gospel unless somehow we can nourish and
preserve the results.

Clarence W. Jones (TET)

❖ ❖ ❖

Both discipleship and church planting are of vital
importance; to have one without the other skews the
results. Both must exist as a part of a goal-oriented
process that includes new disciples and new churches.

Derek Seipp (EGK, 118)

❖ ❖ ❖

The only way to ensure that the national churches are
not dependent on outside missionaries forever is not
for them to step out of the picture, but rather to be
obedient to 2 Timothy 2:2. We must train trainers,
teach teachers, and disciple disciplers. It is clear that
national churches should not become dependent on
our money, but Jesus commands us to teach. Yes, we
have taught them for years, but before we leave, we
must teach others to teach so that they can continue
the task.

David Sills (R&T, 26–27)

Biblical mission demands that those who claim Christ's name should be like him, by taking up their cross, denying themselves, and following him in the paths of humility, love, integrity, generosity, and servanthood. To fail in discipleship and disciple-making, is to fail at the most basic level of our mission. The call of Christ to his church comes to us afresh from the pages of the Gospels "come and follow me"; "go and make disciples."

Cape Town Commitment (CTC, 71)

Our final work as a witness is not leading someone to make the decision to ask Christ into his or her heart, but guiding that person into the life of Christian discipleship. This way of living involves an ongoing journey toward maturity that is marked by several basic commitments needed to discover more of God, to nurture a more Christ-like character and to act in the power of the Holy Spirit.

Daniel Meyer (WE, 209)

Following Jesus, we move from our foundational communion with God into the mission field of an ill and injured world. Focusing on building redemptive relationships, we invest substantial time in people, express authentic affection for them, and gaze with both compassion and humility upon the damage done by sin to human health. These genuine friendships create the indispensable context for further influence.

Daniel Meyer (WE, 88)

❖ ❖ ❖

There is no greater transforming power than the translation of the gospel message and entrusting that message to the work of the Holy Spirit in the local people. Even the best-intended missionary efforts at social development can smack of colonialism and culturally taint or even emasculate the gospel. But as, so to speak, the lion of the gospel is set loose among a people, then personal, ecclesial, and community change occurs in dramatic and unexpected ways.

Craig Ott (ETM, 146)

Discipleship means adherence to Christ, and,
because Christ is the object of that adherence, it
must take the form of discipleship. An abstract
Christology, a doctrinal system, a general religious
knowledge on the subject of grace or on the
forgiveness of sins, render discipleship superfluous.

Dietrich Bonhoeffer (TCOD, 63)

❖ ❖ ❖

Christ is either Lord of all, or is not Lord at all.

J. Hudson Taylor (HTLD, 57)

ETERNAL DESTINY

The seventeenth century preacher, Samuel Rutherford, once told a person, "I would lay my dearest joys in the gap between you and eternal destruction." Hudson Taylor said, "I would have never thought of going to China had I not believed that the Chinese were lost and needed Christ." D. L. Moody told an audience in London, "If I believed there was no hell, I am sure I would be off tomorrow for America." He said he would gladly give up going from town to town spending day and night "urging men to escape the damnation of hell." William Booth said he would wish that his Salvation Army workers might spend "one night in hell" in order to see the urgency of their evangelistic task.

———

Ajith Fernando (PB)

For Christ's sake we Christians care about all suffering, especially eternal suffering. I don't want you to choose between these two truths. Christ doesn't want you to choose between pouring your life out for the alleviation of unjust human suffering now and the pouring out of your life to rescue the perishing from everlasting suffering, which is 10 million times worse than anything anybody will ever experience here. I don't want you to choose between these two. Christ is calling us to pull these together.

John Piper (JP1)

❖   ❖   ❖

If we lose the doctrine of hell, either too embarrassed to mention it or too culturally sensitive to affirm it, we can count on this: the boat will drift. The cross will be stripped of propitiation, our preaching will be devoid of urgency and power, and our work in the world will no longer center on calling people to faith and repentance and building them to maturity in Christ. Lose the ballast of divine judgment and our message, our ministry, and our mission will all change eventually.

Kevin Deyoung and Greg Gilbert (WMC, 245)

The Lord will be my judge someday. I will give an account to him of how I served him. I expect that as he goes down the list of the choices I have made, none will have a perfectly pure motivation, and many will appear as unwise in the bright light of his holiness. I hope I have been a good steward of my gifts and time. But my confidence in the judgment is not in that. It's in the perfection of Jesus that God has credited to me through faith and in the punishment Jesus endured for me. And I believe there will be in my overall ministry sufficient, imperfect fruits of love that witness that my union with Jesus by faith was real.

———

John Piper (JP4, 39)

❖ ❖ ❖

Would that God would make hell so real to us that we cannot rest; heaven so real that we must have men there; Christ so real that our supreme motive and aim shall be to make the Man of Sorrows, the Man of Joy by the conversion to Him of many.

———

J. Hudson Taylor (TGE, 79)

Since hell is real, we must help each other die well
even more than we strive to help our neighbors
live comfortably. Since hell is real, we must never
think alleviating earthly suffering is the most loving
thing we can do. Since hell is real, evangelism
and discipleship are not simply good options or
commendable ministries, but are literally a matter of
life and death.

Kevin Deyoung and Greg Gilbert (WMC, 245)

❖ ❖ ❖

If there rises in your heart a resistance to the phrases
especially "eternal suffering," or if there rises in
your heart a resistance to the phrase, "we care about
all suffering now"; if resistance rises to either one
of those, either we have a defective view of hell or a
defective heart.

John Piper (JP1)

❖ ❖ ❖

I have discovered that the people who believe most
strongly in the next life do the most good in the
present one.

C. S. Lewis (DCQ)

EVANGELISM
(WITNESS)

Wherever we go, we either bring people nearer
to Christ, or we repel them from Christ. We are
working for the great kingdom of God—the time
when all people will turn to Christ as their leader—
and will not be afraid to own him as such.

Eric Liddell (EMQ3)

❖ ❖ ❖

It is possible for the most obscure person in a church,
with a heart right toward God, to exercise as much
power for the evangelization of the world, as it is for
those who stand in the most prominent positions.

John R. Mott (SNU)

Oh give thanks to the Lord; call upon his name;
make known his deeds among the peoples!

(Psalm 105:1)

❖ ❖ ❖

To stop or linger anywhere, even to repeat the
rejected message, so long as there are souls beyond
that have never heard it, is at least unjust to those who
are still in absolute darkness.

A. T. Pierson (ETM, 111)

❖ ❖ ❖

Evangelism is not correct theory. Evangelism is
seeking and saving sinners. Evangelism is not
correct theology—though the closer evangelism
remains to the truths of the Christian revelation,
the more it will please God. Evangelism is finding
lost children of God and bringing them rejoicing
into the household of God. Evangelism is bringing
lost men to the Savior.

Donald McGavran (CED, 66)

The church which ceases to be evangelistic will soon cease to be evangelical.

Alexander Duff (DCQ)

❖ ❖ ❖

In fields white to harvest, evangelism is each bringing his quota of sheaves to the Master's threshing floor. Evangelism is not a nice weighing of rights and wrongs. Evangelism is an overwhelming conviction of the preeminence of Christ flowing through human life like a river in flood.

Donald McGavran (CED, 66)

❖ ❖ ❖

It has always been my ambition to preach the gospel where Christ was not known, so that I would not be building on someone else's foundation. Rather as it is written, "Those who were not told about him will see, and those who have not heard will understand."

Apostle Paul (Rom 15:20–21)

Remember, a small light will do a great deal when it is in a very dark place. Put one little tallow candle in the middle of a large hall, and it will give a good deal of light.

D. L. Moody (DLM1)

❖ ❖ ❖

The tendency among some evangelicals to downplay verbal proclamation—including persuading people to receive Christ's salvation—demands a fresh call for evangelicals to emphasize the urgency of proactive evangelism. And if talk of priority will help the church to a fresh commitment, then so be it.

Craig Ott (ETM, 146)

❖ ❖ ❖

At the moment I put the bread and wine into those dark hands, once stained with the blood of cannibalism, now stretched out to receive and partake the emblems and seals of the Redeemer's love, I had a foretaste of the joy of glory that well nigh broke my heart to pieces. I shall never taste a deeper bliss, till I gaze on the glorified face of Jesus himself.

John G. Paton (TET)

The scope of God's purpose (in telling Abraham
his plans) must be carefully noted. His will, as
made known to Abraham, bound all Abraham's
descendants. Certainly God does not make his will
known to us so that knowledge of him should die
with us. He requires us to be his witnesses to the next
generation, so that they may in turn hand on what
they have received from us to their descendants. ...
In this way we must propagate God's truth. It was not
given for our private enjoyment; we must mutually
strengthen one another according to our calling and
our faith.

John Calvin (MGP, 83)

❖   ❖   ❖

I have known them to stand listening for hours and
night after night, when we ceased preaching to go
home, I have heard one hundred to two hundred
men cry out, "Stay and tell us more!" It is no
weariness to the flesh to tell our gospel to people
so willing to hear. Time flies and our strength is
renewed like the eagle's.

Jonathan Goforth (EMQ5, 158)

The missionary as an ambassador for Christ becomes
a herald of truth. When Jesus sent out the twelve
apostles on their first preaching mission He gave
them clear instructions: "What I tell you in the dark,
utter in the light, and what you hear whispered,
proclaim upon the housetops" (Matt 10:27). The
idea of a herald is that of a town crier before days of
mass communications. He marched the length and
breadth of the town reading aloud a proclamation
for the benefit of the townsfolk. He did not invent
or originate the message. He simply proclaimed it.
This is the responsibility of the missionary. He does
not invent his message any more than Paul did (Gal
1:1–10). He has been told precisely what he is to teach
and preach: all that Jesus commanded (Matt 28:20).
That includes all His major discourses, public and
private, including the Sermon on the Mount.

J. Herbert Kane (UCM, 32)

❖ ❖ ❖

Without the accompanying deeds, the good news is
scarcely credible; without the word, the news is not
even comprehensible!

Samuel H. Moffett (PWCM, 576)

Don't confuse your foundation (the church) with
your mission field (those outside of the church).
Don't let the good you experience in the life of the
community of faith distract you from the Great
Commission Christ has given all believers, including
you. It's fine to pray for more people to come into
our fellowships, but Jesus suggests that the bulk of
our prayer ought to be for more of the church to go
out walking, as he did, in the fields of this world.

Daniel Meyer (WE, 96)

❖ ❖ ❖

Declare his glory among the nations, his marvelous
works among all the peoples! For great is the Lord,
and greatly to be praised, and he is to be feared above
all gods.

King David (1 Chr 16:24–25)

❖ ❖ ❖

It is always true in the work of evangelization that
the present can never anticipate the future, and the
future can never replace the past. What is to be done
in soul saving must be done by that generation.

J. Oswald Sanders (TGE, 120)

Evangelism must be an obsession. The basic element in mission outreach is the primary place of evangelism, not just in word but in deed. Evangelism was the direct command of Jesus to His disciples; it is the commission to the church. Other ministries should reinforce evangelism, not replace it. Over-specialization and institutionalism have tended to deflect from pioneer evangelism.

Jack Frizen (IFMA, 391)

❖ ❖ ❖

Jesus has both called and empowered us to take our place among the great cloud of witnesses God is using to advance his redemptive purposes in history. The question that naturally arises is How? How do we go about being these witnesses of whom Jesus speaks? The short answer to this question is, "by proclaiming the gospel message."

Daniel Meyer (WE, 41)

FAITH

Christ wants not nibblers of the possible, but grabbers of the impossible.

C. T. Studd (SNU)

❖ ❖ ❖

The use of means ought not to lessen our faith in God, and our faith in God ought not hinder our using whatever means he has given us for the accomplishment of his own purposes.

J. Hudson Taylor (WHT, chapter 8)

❖ ❖ ❖

Unless there is the element of extreme risk in our exploits for God, there is no need for faith.

J. Hudson Taylor (TET)

It is a tragedy when a man has no invisible means
of support.

T. J. Bach (PMS, 41)

True faith glories in the present tense, and does not
trouble itself about the future. God's promises are
in the present tense, and are quite secure enough to
set our hearts at rest. Their full outworking is often
in the future, but God's word is as good as His bond
and we need have no anxiety.

James O. Fraser (OMF)

Expect great things; Attempt great things.

William Carey (SHY, 14)

FAMILY

Marriage can be a great blessing or a great curse, depending upon where you place the Cross.

C. T. Studd (F&F, 64)

❖ ❖ ❖

God is not calling us to win the world and, in the process, lose our families. But I have known those who so enshrined family life and were so protective of "quality time" that the children never saw in their parents the kind of consuming love that made their parent's faith attractive to them. Some have lost their children, not because they weren't at their soccer games or didn't take family vacations, but because they never transmitted a loyalty to Jesus that went deep enough to interrupt personal preferences.

David Shibley (EMT)

The perils of missionary pioneers were shared by the pioneer wives. Judson in his prison, Moffatt with his savages in South Africa, Chalmers in the wilderness of New Guinea, Hunt and Calvert in blood-stained Fiji, Paton in New Hebrides, all these and hundreds more had some woman who stood shoulder to shoulder with them, sharing weariness, danger, loneliness, sickness, death.

Helen Barrett Montgomery (WWEL, 158)

❖ ❖ ❖

The safest place for yourself and the children is in the path of duty.

Jonathan Goforth (HIK, 83)

❖ ❖ ❖

If such exquisite delights as we have enjoyed … with one another, are allowed to sinful creatures on earth, what must the joys of heaven be?

Adoniram Judson, to his wife (MFL, 116)

GIVING

Depend on it. God's work done in God's way will never lack God's supply. He is too wise a God to frustrate His purposes for lack of funds, and He can just as easily supply them ahead of time as afterwards, and He much prefers doing so.

J. Hudson Taylor (PFI, 37)

❖ ❖ ❖

Is not the festive season when families and friends exchange gifts in memory of The Gift laid on the altar of the world for the redemption of the human race, the most appropriate time to consecrate a portion from abounding riches and scant poverty to send forth the good tidings of great joy into all the earth?

Lottie Moon (IMB)

HOW MUCH SHALL I GIVE?

1. If I refuse to give anything to missions this year, I practically cast a ballot in favor of the recall of every missionary.
2. If I give less than heretofore, I favor reduction of the missionary forces proportionate to my reduced contribution.
3. If I give the same as formerly, I favor holding the ground already won; but I oppose any forward movement. My song is "Hold the Fort," forgetting that the Lord never intended His army to take refuge in a fort. All His soldiers are commanded to "Go."
4. If I increase my offering beyond former years, then I favor an advance movement in the conquest of new territory for Christ.

Unknown (BMM, 833)

❖ ❖ ❖

People don't give to meet a need; they give to support a vision! Convey your burden with conviction. Convey your burden with emotion. Convey your burden with sincerity. Convey your burden with confidence.

William P. Dillon (PR, 120)

GIVING

People give to people.
People give to people they know.
People give to people they know and trust.
People give to people they know, trust, and care for.

William P. Dillon (PR, 57)

❖ ❖ ❖

Do not think me mad. It is not to make money that
I believe a Christian should live. The noblest thing
a man can do is, just humbly to receive, and then go
amongst others and give.

David Livingstone (TTT)

GOAL OF MISSIONS

The goal of Christian missions is not limited to mere physical presence among unbelievers nor to the verbal proclamation of the gospel among those who have never heard it. It is not limited to establishing a network of mission stations across a defined geographical area. Neither is it confined to dotting the countryside of a given nation with a series of preaching points of developing Bible study groups in scattered urban neighborhoods. Nor is it restricted to the conversion of individual persons. The goal of missions is to establish within every people group in the world, within every piece of the human mosaic, indigenous church movements which are capable of so multiplying congregations that the entire people group is both evangelized and incorporated into the fellowship of the church.

Kenneth B. Mulholland (PWCM, 136)

For the earth will be filled with the knowledge of the glory of the Lord as the waters cover the sea.

Prophet Habakkuk (Hab 2:14)

❖ ❖ ❖

The infinite, all-glorious Creator of the universe, by whom and for whom all things exist—who holds every person's life in being at every moment (Acts 17:25)—is disregarded, disbelieved, disobeyed, and dishonored among the peoples of the world. That is the ultimate reason for missions.

John Piper (LNBG, 206)

❖ ❖ ❖

Missions is the overflow of our delight in God because missions is the overflow of God's delight in being God. And the deepest reason why worship is the goal in missions is that worship is God's goal. We are confirmed in this goal by the biblical record of God's relentless pursuit of praise among the nations. "Praise the Lord, all nations! Extol him, all peoples!" (Ps 117:1). If it is God's goal it must be our goal.

John Piper (LNBG, 21)

To this end the King has given orders to His
ambassadors. They are to go into all the world,
preach the gospel to every creature, and make
disciples of all nations (Matt 28:19). All men
everywhere are required to repent and believe the
gospel (Acts 17:30). Only by so doing can they be
delivered from the dominion of darkness and be
transferred to the kingdom of light (Col 1:13).
Nothing short of world conquest is the ultimate goal,
and the King has given assurance that one day the
kingdoms of this world are to become the Kingdom
of our Lord and of His Christ (Rev 11:15). There is
no ambiguity about the plan, no uncertainty about
the outcome.

J. Herbert Kane (UCM, 31)

❖ ❖ ❖

The world to come at the end of history will be
a world without the national barriers that divide
people today, a glorious and rich mosaic of peoples,
languages, and cultures around the Lamb of God.
Missionary internationalization is a clear step in that
direction.

Samuel Escobar (TGE, 47)

And this gospel of the kingdom will be proclaimed throughout the whole world as a testimony to all nations, and then the end will come.

Jesus (Matt 24:14)

❖   ❖   ❖

What is the result of the gospel? Surely something more than every person having a chance to pass verdict on the message. God has promised to get obedient glory for Himself from every tribe and tongue. He yearns for the unique outpouring of love, righteousness, wisdom and worship that can come from every people. This would be the best rationale for planting indigenous churches. Such a vantage point elevates the distinctive wonder of each people group, and at the same time, enhances the value of extending the gospel breakthrough to every place.

Steven C. Hawthorne (PWCM, 62)

❖   ❖   ❖

The aim of the missionary is to do God's will, not to be useful, not to win the heathen; he is useful and does win the heathen, but that is not his aim. His aim is to do the will of his Lord.

Oswald Chambers (TMC, 45)

The promise linked to the commission is "to the very end of the age." This clearly indicates that the commission is to continue until Christ's return and this eon comes to an end. The promise does not end with the death of the first-generation disciples, nor does the commission. The commission fills the time between Christ's comings, ushering in the completion of salvation history. Only when the gospel has been preached to every nation will the end come (Matt 24:14).

Craig Ott (ETM, 37)

GOD & MISSIONS

Here [Psalm 96] we arrive at the fundamental equation of mission, the driving force behind all our efforts to bring the news of the one true Lord to our friends and neighbours: If there is one Lord to whom all people belong and owe their allegiance, the people of that Lord must promote this reality everywhere. Monotheism and mission are intimately related. The existence of just one God makes our mission to the many essential.

John Dickson (MGP, 159)

❖ ❖ ❖

We must be global Christians with a global vision because our God is a global God.

John R. W. Stott (PWCM, 9)

The nations are not gathered in automatically. If God has promised to bless "all the families of the earth," he has promised to do so "through Abraham's seed" (Gen 12:3, 22:18). Now we are Abraham's seed by faith, and the earth's families will be blessed only if we go to them with the gospel. That is God's plain purpose.

John R. W. Stott (PWCM, 9)

❖ ❖ ❖

God is the God of missions. He wills missions. He commands missions. He demands missions. He made missions possible through His Son. He made missions actual in sending the Holy Spirit. Biblical Christianity and missions are organically interrelated.

George W. Peters (BTM, 346)

❖ ❖ ❖

Those who know God's history can better lay hold of God's intended purposes.

Ralph Winter (FWCM)

There is none like you among the gods, O Lord,
nor are there any works like yours. All the nations
you have made shall come and worship before you,
O Lord, and shall glorify your name. For you are
great and do wondrous things; you alone are God.

King David (Ps 86:8–10)

❖ ❖ ❖

Belief in God as Trinity is the cornerstone of the
Christian faith. Without it we would have a creator
God who is distant and impersonal, a Jesus who
was merely an outstanding historical figure—a mere
human being, and a Spirit who would be thought of
as only an arbitrary natural force. Without belief in
Trinity we have a deficient view of God, which in turn
makes for a deficient presentation of the gospel.

M. Newell (MJN, 99)

❖ ❖ ❖

God proved His love on the cross. When Christ
hung, and bled, and died, it was God saying to the
world, "I love you."

Billy Graham (BG)

Not only subjective obedience to mission, but also the entire objective existence of mission is rooted in the certainty that God is the origin of mission. The same divine authority that mothered the very thought of mission is also the only power that can drive the will for missionary service (John 10:16; 1 Cor 9:16ff.; Rom 1:14; Gal 1:16) and offer the sure foundation and guaranty for the success of mission.

Gustav Warneck (ETM, 62)

❖ ❖ ❖

The God who made the world and everything in it, being Lord of heaven and earth, does not live in temples made by man, nor is he served by human hands, as though he needed anything, since he himself gives to all mankind life and breath and everything. And he made from one man every nation of mankind to live on all the face of the earth, having determined allotted periods and the boundaries of their dwelling place, that they should seek God, and perhaps feel their way toward him and find him. Yet he is actually not far from each one of us, for "'In him we live and move and have our being'; as even some of your own poets have said, "'For we are indeed his offspring.'

Apostle Paul (Acts 17:24–28)

The mission of God flows from the love of God.
The mission of God's people flows from our love for
God and for all that God loves. World evangelization
is the outflow of God's love to us and through us.
We affirm the primacy of God's grace and we then
respond to that grace by faith, demonstrated through
the obedience of love. We love because God first
loved us and sent his Son to be the propitiation for
our sins.

Cape Town Commitment (CTC, 9)

❖ ❖ ❖

Learning to follow God's ways may be more
important than making sincere attempts to do His
will. God is eager to reveal His ways to us because
they are the only way to accomplish His purposes.
God wants to complete His work through you. He
can only do that as you adjust your life to Him and
to His ways. Start looking for how God welcomes
you to join Him and to experience Him. He has
involved His people on mission with Him in the
same ways all through history.

Henry Blackaby (MF1)

Give thanks to the Lord, call upon his name, make known his deeds among the peoples, proclaim that his name is exalted. Sing praises to the Lord, for he has done gloriously; let this be made known in all the earth. Shout, and sing for joy, O inhabitant of Zion, for great in your midst is the Holy One of Israel.

Prophet Isaiah (Isa 12:4–6)

❖   ❖   ❖

Don't wait for a feeling of love in order to share Christ with a stranger. You already love your heavenly Father, and you know that this stranger is created by Him, but separated from Him, so take those first steps in evangelism because you love God. It is not primarily out of a compassion for humanity that we share our faith or pray for the lost; it is first of all, love for God. The Bible says in Ephesians 6:7–8: "With good will doing service, as to the Lord, and not to men, knowing that whatever good anyone does, he will receive the same from the Lord, whether he is a slave or free."

John Dawson (TCFG, 208–209)

The ultimate issue addressed by missions is that God's glory is dishonored among the peoples of the world. When Paul brought his indictment of his own people to a climax in Romans 2:24, he said, "The name of God is blasphemed among the Gentiles because of you." That is the ultimate problem in the world. That is the ultimate outrage.

The glory of God is not honored.
The holiness of God is not reverenced.
The greatness of God is not admired.
The power of God is not praised.
The truth of God is not sought.
The wisdom of God is not esteemed.
The beauty of God is not treasured.
The goodness of God is not savored.
The faithfulness of God is not trusted.
The commandments of God are not obeyed.
The justice of God is not feared.
The grace of God is not cherished.
The presence of God is not prized.
The person of God is not loved.

John Piper (LNBG, 206)

When God spoke to us in Scripture he used human language, and when he spoke to us in Christ he assumed human flesh. In order to reveal himself, he both emptied and humbled himself. That is the model of evangelism which the Bible supplies. There is self-emptying and self-humbling in all authentic evangelism; without it we contradict the gospel and misrepresent the Christ we proclaim.

John R. W. Stott (PWCM, 24)

❖ ❖ ❖

The end product of evangelism is not just to get you out of hell and into heaven, but to get God out of heaven and into you, so that Christ living in your heart might bring God out again into the open where He can be seen. This is what brings glory to God.

Major Ian Thomas (ILC, 92)

❖ ❖ ❖

Christian missions are no human undertaking, but a supernatural and divine enterprise for which God has provided supernatural power and leadership.

Robert H. Glover (RHG, 70)

108

In seeking to fulfill Jesus' command, his disciples will not always succeed. They will not always be able to persuade others; their judgment will be faulty; they will not be fully free from the taint of sin; physical weakness will thwart them; what men call death will come, early or late, to cut off the act before its final accomplishment, so far beyond the compass of human years has it been planned. Yet it is through daring to live now in the new age and not resting content until all their fellow creatures share it that God brings in his Kingdom. He is not ashamed to be called their God. In the eternity beyond this present span, we must believe, they will not be disappointed, for they have ventured out in faith in him who is "able to do far more abundantly than all that we ask or think."

Kenneth Scott Latourette (KSL, 147)

❖ ❖ ❖

God's supervision is so blessedly true that at any given moment ... whatever we may face we may say, "For this cause came I unto this hour."

John Stam (EMQ3)

All the ends of the earth shall remember
and turn to the Lord,
and all the families of the nations
shall worship before you.
For kingship belongs to the Lord,
and he rules over the nations.
All the prosperous of the earth eat and worship;
before him shall bow all who go down to the dust,
even the one who could not keep himself alive.
Posterity shall serve him;
it shall be told of the Lord to the coming generation;
they shall come and proclaim his righteousness to a
people yet unborn,
that he has done it.

King David (Ps 22:27–31)

❖   ❖   ❖

The man ... looking at him with a smile that only
half concealed his contempt, inquired, "Now, Mr.
Morrison, do you really expect that you will make an
impression on the idolatry of the Chinese Empire?"
"No sir," said Morrison, "but I expect that God will."

Robert Morrison (MHMF, 104)

110

This, then, is the biblical basis for missions: World evangelization is the expressed will of God. Spiritual redemption is the demonstrated activity of God. Evangelism and redemptive activity are expressed as the will of God and the demonstrated activity of God because it is the nature of God so to will and so to act. Love is the revealed nature of God. The salvation of lost men is that human event which brings greatest glory to God.

Robertson McQuilkin (TGO, 37)

❖   ❖   ❖

If all people on earth could prosper and be given a college education, full employment prevailed, all injustice and warfare ceased, and perfect health prevailed, but people remained alienated from God, his father heart would still be broken. His priority for alienated human beings is reconciliation to himself.

Robertson McQuilkin (ETM, 146)

❖   ❖   ❖

When I am gone, say nothing about Dr. Carey. Speak about Dr. Carey's Savior.

William Carey (SQB, 67)

111

Thus even in the most elementary form the
preaching of the Gospel must presuppose an
understanding of the triune nature of God. It is
not, as we have sometimes seemed to say, a kind
of intellectual capstone which can be put on to
the top of the arch at the very end; it is, on the
contrary, what Athanasius called it, the *arche*, the
presupposition without which the preaching of the
Gospel in a pagan world cannot begin.

Lesslie Newbigin (ETM, 36)

❖ ❖ ❖

Oh sing to the Lord a new song;
sing to the Lord, all the earth!
Sing to the Lord, bless his name;
tell of his salvation from day to day.
Declare his glory among the nations,
his marvelous works among all the peoples!
For great is the Lord, and greatly to be praised;
he is to be feared above all gods.
For all the gods of the peoples are worthless idols,
but the Lord made the heavens.
Splendor and majesty are before him;
strength and beauty are in his sanctuary.

Psalm 96:1–6

It is remarkable that God began this work among the Indians at a time when I had the least hope, and to my apprehension the least rational prospect of success.

David Brainerd (WJE, 399)

❖ ❖ ❖

Missionaries who make a mark in our unpredictable world will be those who learn best how to follow the sovereign, all-wise Christ through unexpected twists and turns and bone-jarring potholes, instead of becoming frustrated, disillusioned, or sidetracked. ... And when we pray for the missionaries we've already sent out and supported, let's add to our prayers for safety, strength, and souls, one more strategic request: a prayer for flexibility.

Ken Mauger (MC1)

HOLY SPIRIT & MISSIONS

Pastors and congregations must be led to study the Pentecostal pattern. We should be content with nothing less than an equal devotion to the work of making Christ known everywhere. The only power to evangelize the world in this generation lies in knowing what Pentecost means and to have its faith and its Spirit.

Andrew Murray (AM, 82)

❖ ❖ ❖

How little chance the Holy Ghost has nowadays. The churches and missionary societies have so bound him in red tape that they practically ask Him to sit in a corner while they do the work themselves.

C. T. Studd (TTT)

Why do so many workers break down? Not from overwork, but because there has been friction of the machinery; there hasn't been enough oil of the Spirit.

D. L. Moody (LAI, 86)

❖ ❖ ❖

I do not know how to make a man think seriously about sin and judgment, and must look to the work of the Holy Spirit for any hint of such a working.

Jim Elliot (TET)

❖ ❖ ❖

Missionaries and nationals are agreed "that the world's evangelization is a divine enterprise, that the Spirit of God is the great Missioner, and that only as he dominates the work and workers can we hope for success in the undertaking to carry the knowledge of Christ to all people. They believe that he gave the missionary impulse to the early church, and that today all true mission work must be inaugurated, directed and sustained by Him."

John R. Mott, 1910 (ETM, 76)

What we need to be assured of is not that we possess an excellent system of doctrine and ritual, but that the gift of the Holy Spirit is a reality.

Roland Allen (TET)

❖ ❖ ❖

Spiritual preparation for evangelism recognizes that the Spirit of God is the Great Persuader of men's hearts. What do you know personally of the Holy Spirit working in and through you? Learn from him to "walk in the light" with the roof off between you and God, and the walls down between you and your brothers.

Warren Webster (WW2)

❖ ❖ ❖

Whatever else you fail of, do not fail of the influences of the Holy Spirit; that is the only way you can handle the consciences of men.

David Brainerd (SMP, 18)

Human Condition
(Lostness)

All the wretchedness in this world has its origin in what this cursed, hellish pride—either our own, or that of others—has brought us. All wars and bloodshed among the nations, all selfishness and suffering, all ambitions and jealousies, all broken hearts and embittered lives, with all the daily unhappiness, are a result of this same wicked pride. It is pride that made redemption necessary. It is from our pride we need, above everything, to be redeemed.

Andrew Murray (AM1, 24)

❖   ❖   ❖

Lost people matter to God, and so they must matter to us.

Keith Wright (GMN)

Behind the shameful apathy and lethargy of the
church, that allows one thousand million …
human beings to go to their graves in ignorance of
the gospel, there lies a practical doubt, if not denial,
of their lost condition.

A. T. Pierson (TGE, 73)

❖ ❖ ❖

There is a God-shaped vacuum in the heart of every
man which cannot be filled by any created thing, but
only by God, the Creator, made known through Jesus.

Blaise Pascal (GRQ)

❖ ❖ ❖

It is to be kept in mind that the "generations" of men
do not wait for the convenience of the church in
respect to their evangelization. Men are born and die
whether or not Christians are ready to give them the
gospel. And hence, if the church of any generation
does not evangelize the heathen of that generation,
those heathen will never be evangelized at all.

J. Oswald Sanders (TGE, 120)

Man has two great spiritual needs.
One is for forgiveness.
The other is for goodness.

———

Billy Graham (THS)

❖　❖　❖

If this indeed is the present condition and future
prospect of the heathen—and Scripture seems to
offer no alternative—and if the church of Christ has
in her charge the message which alone can transform
these tragic "withouts" into the possession of "the
unsearchable riches of Christ," then how urgent is
the missionary enterprise. And how great the tragedy
if we fail to proclaim it.

———

J. Oswald Sanders (JOS, 124)

❖　❖　❖

If this view is correct (universalism), the logical but
unthinkable result will be that Judas and Pilate, Nero
and Hitler will eventually fraternize in heaven with
Paul and Augustine, Wesley and Moody.

———

J. Oswald Sanders (JOS)

It breaks your heart to meet people who have never heard the good news about Jesus Christ but who have learned to swear in his name from secular internationals.

J. Christy Wilson (JCW)

❖ ❖ ❖

To an age which has unashamedly sold itself to the gods of greed, pride, sex, and self-will, the church mumbles on about God's kindness, but says virtually nothing about His judgment. ... The fact is that the subject of divine wrath has become taboo in modern society, and Christians by and large have accepted the taboo and conditioned themselves never to raise the subject.

J. I. Packer (JIP)

❖ ❖ ❖

As long as there are millions destitute of the Word of God and knowledge of Jesus Christ, it will be impossible for me to devote time and energy to those who have both.

J. L. Ewen (BSWE)

If people are cut off from eternal life (Eph 2:2–3,12; 4:17; 5:6), and if calling on Jesus is their only hope for eternal, joyful fellowship with God … then love demands missions. The biggest problem in the world for every human being—from the poorest to the richest, from the sickest to the healthiest—is the same: how to escape the wrath of God that hangs over all humans because of our sin. Love demands that we work to rescue people from the wrath of God.

John Piper (ETM, 179)

❖   ❖   ❖

When all has been said that can be said on this issue (of the lost), the greatest remaining mystery is not the character of God nor the destiny of lost people. The greatest mystery is why those who are charged with rescuing the lost have spent two thousand years doing other things, good things, perhaps, but have failed to send and be sent until all have heard the liberating word of life in Christ Jesus. The lost condition of human beings breaks the Father's heart. What does it do to ours?

Robertson McQuilkin (PWCM, 160–161)

At the end of the earth, people often come to the end of themselves. No one can come here without facing the crushing truth that the bad news is about as bad as it can be—mankind has a cancer of the soul that is incurable and eternally fatal. Fortunately, understanding that fact is also what makes the Good News so good.

Michael G. Loftis (ML)

❖ ❖ ❖

But is it fair and just for God to condemn those who have not had an opportunity to respond to His offer of grace? The Bible does not teach that God will judge a person for rejecting Christ if he has not heard of Christ. In fact, the Bible teaches clearly that God's judgment is based on a person's response to the truth he has received. Judgment is against a person in proportion to his rejection of moral light. All have sinned; no one is innocent. Therefore, all stand condemned. But not all have the same measure of condemnation, for not all have sinned against equal amounts of light. God does not condemn a person who has not heard of Christ for rejecting Him, but rather for rejecting the light he does have.

Robertson McQuilkin (PWCM, 159)

It has been well for me to remember, when speaking to others, that I am a dying man speaking to dying souls.

T. J. Bach (GDE)

❖　❖　❖

Dr. George Peters told of a fellow student who asked their professor, "What is God going to do with those people who die in ignorance?" The professor sat for a moment, his eyes becoming glassy with tears, then he said, "Brother, that I have to leave to God. But, I have an even more serious question. What is God going to do with the church that leaves them in ignorance?"

Jack Frizen (IFMA, 391)

❖　❖　❖

Do not suppose that God or His people will turn sinners out of heaven and cast them into hell, for God who is Love, never cast anyone into hell, nor ever will do so. It is the foul life of the sinner that will bring him to hell. Long before the end of life brings heaven and hell near to us, there has been set up in every man's heart, according to his good or evil nature, his own heaven or hell.

Sadhu Sundar Singh (ETM, 296)

Men are in this plight not because they are unevangelized, but because they are men. Sin is the destroyer of the soul and the destruction of the knowledge of God which is life. And it is not the failure to have heard the gospel which makes men sinners. The gospel would save them if they heard it and accepted it, but it is not the ignorance or rejection of the gospel which destroys them, it is the knowledge of sin.

Robert E. Speer (RES)

HUMAN INSTRUMENTALITY

Your story is always going to be about advancing
God's story. ... Ask yourself: How does God intend
to use me to extend His grace and demonstrate His
glory to all peoples? When you discover how God is
uniquely committed to pouring His grace into your
life, you will be well on your way to discovering how
He intends to pour His grace through your life.

John Kitchen (LSS, 200)

❖ ❖ ❖

I used to ask God to help me.
Then I asked if I might help Him.
I ended up by asking Him
to do His work through me.

J. Hudson Taylor (AG, 150)

Jesus Christ alone can save the world, but Jesus Christ cannot save the world alone.

George Sherwood Eddy (SPMC, 12)

❖ ❖ ❖

Do all the good that you can, by all the means you can, in all the ways you can, in all the places you can, at all the times you can, to all the people you can, as long as ever you can.

John Wesley (JW)

❖ ❖ ❖

The living God, maker of heaven and earth, lover of our souls, the eternal Father, sends his people on a mission in this world. Having redeemed us by the blood of his Son, having given us his message in the Bible, and having equipped us with the Holy Spirit, he sends us to become his instruments for fulfilling his purposes in history. The more one contemplates this thought, the more awe inspiring and overwhelming it becomes; the deeper our sense of privilege, unworthiness, and inadequacy, the greater the urgency to make sure that we get it right.

Craig Ott (ETM, xi)

Men are God's method. The church is looking for better methods; God is looking for better men. ... What the church needs today is not more machinery or better, not new organizations or more and novel methods, but men whom the Holy Ghost can use— men of prayer, men mighty in prayer. The Holy Ghost does not come on machinery, but on men. He does not anoint plans, but men—men of prayer. ... The training of the Twelve was the great, difficult and enduring work of Christ. ... It is not great talents or great learning or great preachers that God needs, but men great in holiness, great in faith, great in love, great in fidelity, great for God—men always preaching by holy sermons in the pulpit, by holy lives out of it. These can mold a generation for God.

E. M. Bounds (PTP, chapter 1)

✦ ✦ ✦

The glory of God's will means trust, it means the will to do his will, and it means joy. Can you lose? Certainly you can. Go ahead and lose your life—that's how you find it! What's your life for? "My life," Jesus said, "for the life of the world."

Elisabeth Elliot Leitch, Urbana 1976 address (EEL)

Let us not be content to wait and see what will
happen, but give us the determination to make the
right things happen.

Peter Marshall (QB)

❖   ❖   ❖

It is too light a thing that you should be my servant
to raise up the tribes of Jacob
and to bring back the preserved of Israel;
I will make you as a light for the nations,
that my salvation may reach to the end of the earth.

Prophet Isaiah (Isa 49:6)

❖   ❖   ❖

The nations are not gathered in automatically.
If God has promised to bless "all the families of
the earth," he has promised to do so "through
Abraham's seed" (Gen 12:3; 22:18). Now we are
Abraham's seed by faith, and the earth's families
will be blessed only if we go to them with the gospel.
That is God's plain purpose.

John R. W. Stott (PWCM, 9)

128

Therefore, having this ministry by the mercy of God, we do not lose heart. But we have renounced disgraceful, underhanded ways. We refuse to practice cunning or to tamper with God's word, but by the open statement of the truth we would commend ourselves to everyone's conscience in the sight of God. And even if our gospel is veiled, it is veiled only to those who are perishing. In their case the god of this world has blinded the minds of the unbelievers, to keep them from seeing the light of the gospel of the glory of Christ, who is the image of God. For what we proclaim is not ourselves, but Jesus Christ as Lord, with ourselves as your servants for Jesus' sake. For God, who said, "Let light shine out of darkness," has shone in our hearts to give the light of the knowledge of the glory of God in the face of Jesus Christ. But we have this treasure in jars of clay, to show that the surpassing power belongs to God and not to us.

Apostle Paul (2 Cor 4:1–7)

❖ ❖ ❖

While great stress today is laid on money and methods, men and women are still God's means of reproducing responsible churches.

Vergil Gerber (EGK, 58)

Paul's meaning is that when any nation is favoured with the preaching of the Gospel, it is a pledge and proof of divine love. There is no preacher of the Gospel who has not been raised up by God in His special providence. It is certain, therefore, that God [i.e., God himself, not just the preacher] visits that nation in which the Gospel is proclaimed. ... The Gospel does not fall from the clouds like rain, by accident, but is brought by the hands of men to where God has sent it.

John Calvin (MGP, 202)

❖　❖　❖

If God's glory has captured your vision and His grace now owns your heart, you are unreservedly committed to the same thing that God is utterly devoted to—magnifying His glory and extending His grace to the peoples of the world through the gospel of Jesus Christ. If this is true, God will make your story a part of His story, and whether seemingly large or small, prominent or obscure, powerful or weak, your story will matter. Your life will make a contribution. You will be a part of God's plan. That is all any of us could ever ask, expect or hope. God will make it true.

John Kitchen (LSS, 208)

Edward Judson wrote a book about his father in
which he said that it is a mistake to think that a
second-rate man is good enough to send to the non-
Christian world. "The worst off," he wrote, "need
the very best we have. God gave His best, even His
only begotten Son, in order to redeem a lost world."
He went on to point out that missions have made
their greatest advances when some of the church's
best men and most dedicated scholars have devoted
their talents to the evangelization of the world. Then
he concluded by observing, "It would be a sad day
for American Christians if they should ever deserve
Nehemiah's reproach: 'Their nobles put not their
necks to the work of their Lord.'"

Warren Webster (WW2)

❖　❖　❖

It is always helpful to us to fix our attention on the
God-ward aspect of Christian work; to realize that
the work of God does not mean so much man's work
for GOD, as GOD'S own work through man.

J. Hudson Taylor (JHT, chapter 1)

No less than the first disciples, we are called by Jesus and empowered by his Spirit to play a personally active role in the ultimately unstoppable expansion of Christ's life-redeeming influence, until that coming day when God completes the renewal of his creation. There is no vocation more significant and satisfying than being a witness to the life-changing love of Jesus Christ.

Daniel Meyer (WE, 21)

❖ ❖ ❖

The use of the term missionary. There are those who advocate that we drop the word altogether. Others insist that it should be applied to all committed Christians. Stephen Neill has warned that if everybody is a missionary, nobody is a missionary. The Chinese have a proverb: "If two men feed a horse, it will lose weight; if two men keep a boat, it will soon leak." What is everybody's job is nobody's job. If every Christian is a missionary, missionary work is bound to suffer. It is correct to say that every Christian is, or should be, a witness. It is not correct to say that every Christian is a missionary.

J. Herbert Kane (UCM, 41)

"And I have other sheep that are not of this fold. I must bring them also, and they will listen to my voice. So there will be one flock, one shepherd" (John 10:16). Men cannot hear without a preacher; the other sheep cannot be gathered in unless someone goes out to bring them in. Here is set before us the tremendous missionary task of the Church. And we must not think of that only in terms of what we used to call foreign missions. If we know someone here and now who is outside of his love, we can find him for Christ. The mission of Christ depends on us; it is we who can help him make the world one flock with him as its shepherd.

William Barclay (WB, 66)

JESUS & MISSIONS

God has appointed Christ to be the heir of the world in his kingdom of grace, and to possess and reign over all nations, through the propagation of his gospel, and the power of his Spirit communicating the blessing of it.

Jonathan Edwards (WJE, 285)

❖ ❖ ❖

When you love the Lord, you long to glorify Him and see the nations fall at His feet in worship. When you love your neighbor as yourself, you share the gospel with him and seek to meet his needs in every way you can, which includes seeing him fall at Jesus' feet in thanksgiving for salvation.

David Sills (TMC)

The spirit of Christ is the spirit of missions. The nearer we get to Him, the more intensely missional we become.

Henry Martyn (SNU)

❖ ❖ ❖

Out from the realm of the glory-light
Into the far-away land of night;
Out of the bliss of worshipful song
Into the pain of hatred and wrong;
Out from the holy rapture above
Into the grief of rejected love;
Out from the life at the Father's side
Into the death of the crucified;
Out of high honor and into shame
The Master, willingly, gladly came:
And now, since He may not suffer anew,
As the Father sent Him, so sends He you!

Henry W. Frost, Director China Inland Mission
("Commissioned," BF, 299)

Who is competent, in the last resort, to decide the strategy of Christian missions? Who can tell whether the place of triumphant breakthrough, or the weakest link in the battleline, most needs reinforcements? Only the Commander-In-Chief Himself.

J. N. D. Anderson (TFI, foreword)

❖ ❖ ❖

The Great Commission then, is based on the supremacy and sovereignty of Jesus Christ, the son of God, who in the Incarnation became the Son of Man, that through His death and resurrection He might become the Savior and Sovereign of the world. He is not only the Head of the church and the Lord of the harvest; He is also the Lord of history, the King of the nations, and the Arbiter of human destiny. Sooner or later all men must come to terms with Him. He and He alone has the right to demand universal allegiance.

J. Herbert Kane (UCM)

David Livingstone said, "God had only one Son and He made that Son a missionary." Every missionary follows in the steps of the Son of God, who visited this planet two thousand years ago on a mission of redemption. He came to seek and to save and to give His life a ransom for many. Upon the completion of His mission He returned to His Father in heaven; but before He left He said to His apostles, "As the Father has sent me, even so I send you" (John 20:21). The worldwide mission of the Christian church is rooted in the Incarnation and is part of God's redemptive purpose for the world.

J. Herbert Kane (UCM)

❖ ❖ ❖

As I wander from village to village, I feel it is no idle fancy that the Master walks beside me and I hear his voice saying gently, "I am with you always, even unto the end."

Lottie Moon (TCW, 53)

Jesus is on a mission to redeem the lost and to reconcile all things to himself. He is on a mission to save the planet. He is on a mission to complete the greatest creation of all time, the Body of Christ. He is on a mission to find the lost and broken, make them whole and show them the way home. He is looking for people from every tribe, people, language and nation to be part of the great assembly around the throne. He is setting up his Kingdom in which all those who become his disciples will rule as a Kingdom of priests and a holy nation.

Charles Davis (CD1)

LEADERSHIP

A leader needs to "speak as the oracles of God," which involves a holy fear and trembling as to his own state of heart before God and in relation to his brethren.

———

D. E. Hoste (DEH)

❖ ❖ ❖

Leadership is tested in storms. You may be in the midst of one. ... If not, you will be soon. Storms come with leadership. The names and circumstances are surely different for all of us, but the perplexity and pain are essentially the same.

———

Daniel Henderson (DG, 25)

Leading is inspiring people who participate with you in a community of trust to follow you—a leader or a leadership team—and be empowered by you to achieve a compelling vision of faith.

Sherwood Lingenfelter (LCC, 19)

❖ ❖ ❖

Blessed the man and woman who is able to serve cheerfully in the second rank—a big test.

Mary Slessor (MSC, 298)

❖ ❖ ❖

Leading cross-culturally is inspiring people who come from two or more cultural traditions to participate with you in building a community of trust and then to follow you and be empowered by you to achieve a compelling vision of faith.

Sherwood Lingenfelter (LCC, 21)

❖ ❖ ❖

The best leaders are grown, not grabbed.

Clarence W. Jones (CUTM, 169)

Many Christian leaders are "losing altitude" in ways that most of us do not see or understand. When we "suddenly" hear of a respected executive in our church whose marriage has disintegrated, or a well-known pastor caught in moral indiscretion, we should remember these "crashes" are usually the result of numerous bad decisions made during a long, downward emotional, mental, and spiritual spiral. Sometimes the leader was seeking help during his descent toward disaster. Often it was concealed to everyone.

Daniel Henderson (DG, 36)

❖ ❖ ❖

I myself, for instance, am not especially gifted, and am shy by nature, but my gracious and merciful God and Father inclined Himself to me, and when I was weak in faith He strengthened me while I was still young. He taught me in my helplessness to rest on Him, and to pray even about little things in which another might have felt able to help himself.

J. Hudson Taylor (DCQ-HT)

The vision essential for cross-cultural leadership is based on an understanding of what the Scriptures teach of the kingdom of God and the vision that flows out of the power of the Holy Spirit to establish that kingdom now and in the ages to come.

Sherwood Lingenfelter (LCC, 31)

❖ ❖ ❖

It's amazing what can be accomplished when you don't worry about who gets the credit.

Clarence W. Jones (TTT)

❖ ❖ ❖

The true measure of effective leadership is whether the team does the hard work of loving one another in the midst of disagreement and then pull together to accomplish the will and purpose of God.

Sherwood Lingenfelter (LCC, 66)

LONELINESS

I had feelings of fear about the future. ... The devil
kept on whispering, "It's all right now, but what
about afterwards? You are going to be very lonely."
... And I turned to my God in a kind of desperation
and said, "Lord, what can I do? How can I go on to
the end?" And He said, "None of them that trust in
Me shall be desolate." That word has been with me
ever since.

Amy Carmichael (TUC, 300)

❖ ❖ ❖

Shall I tell you what sustained me amidst the toil,
the hardship, and loneliness of my exiled life? It was
the promise, "Lo, I am with you always, even unto
the end."

David Livingstone (LTP, 136)

At home you can never know what it is to be alone—absolutely alone, amidst thousands, as you can in a Chinese city, without one friend, one companion, everyone looking on you with curiosity, with contempt, with suspicion or with dislike. Thus to learn what it is to be despised and rejected of men—of those you wish to benefit, your motives not understood ... and then to have the love of Jesus applied to your heart by the Holy Spirit ... this is worth coming for.

J. Hudson Taylor (AJB1, 363)

MAN'S RESPONSIBILITY

How do Christians discharge this trust committed
to them? They let three-fourths of the world sleep
the sleep of death, ignorant of the simple truth
that a Savior died for them. Content if they can be
useful in the little circle of their acquaintances, they
quietly sit and see whole nations perish for the lack
of knowledge.

Adoniram Judson (TGE, 69)

❖ ❖ ❖

We may not be able to do any great thing; but if each
of us will do something, however small it may be, a
good deal will be accomplished for God.

D. L. Moody (DLM1, chapter 6)

For "everyone who calls on the name of the Lord will be saved." How then will they call on him in whom they have not believed? And how are they to believe in him of whom they have never heard? And how are they to hear without someone preaching? And how are they to preach unless they are sent? As it is written, "How beautiful are the feet of those who preach the good news!"

Apostle Paul (Rom 10:13—15)

❖ ❖ ❖

Difficult as world evangelization is, our Lord has promised us success. He said, "You shall receive power after the Holy Spirit has come upon you and you shall be witnesses unto me ... unto the uttermost part of the earth" (Acts 1:8). Or as Adoniram Judson Gordon has said, "It is not a matter of bringing the world to Christ; it is a matter of taking Christ to the world."

J. Christy Wilson (JCW)

❖ ❖ ❖

The least difficult thing a foreign missionary has to learn is the language; the part of her work which she has the most reason to dread is its responsibility.

Isabella Thoburn (TET)

Sometimes it may be that while we are complaining of the hardness of hearts of those we are seeking to benefit, that hardness of our own hearts, and our own feeble apprehension of the solemn reality of eternal things, may be the true cause of our want of success.

J. Hudson Taylor (BSWE)

To be an ambassador for Christ, to join his Cause by way of the Great Commission, is what he asks of each of us. No believer should ever feel that he or she is exempt. Jesus will not excuse those who refuse to play even a small part. A widow's mite is just as valuable as a missionary on site.

M. Newell (MJN, 164)

We are debtors to every man to give him the gospel in the same measure in which we have received it.

P. F. Bresee, founder of the Church of the Nazarene (SNU)

It is conceivable that God might have ordained to preach the gospel directly to man through dreams, visions, and revelations. But as a matter of fact he has not done this, but rather has committed the preaching to man, telling them to go and disciple all nations. The responsibility lies squarely on our shoulders.

J. Oswald Sanders (TGE, 33)

Our entire work could be revolutionized ... if we were to major, individually and collectively ... in witnessing, in continuous visitation work, in the sort of personal contacts and friendships which result in reproduction and in the making of disciples.

Kenneth Strachan (EMQ3)

MEANS & MISSION

For though I am free from all, I have made myself a servant to all, that I might win more of them. To the Jews I became as a Jew, in order to win Jews. To those under the law I became as one under the law (though not being myself under the law) that I might win those under the law. To those outside the law I became as one outside the law (not being outside the law of God but under the law of Christ) that I might win those outside the law. To the weak I became weak, that I might win the weak. I have become all things to all people, that by all means I might save some. I do it all for the sake of the gospel, that I may share with them in its blessings.

—————

Apostle Paul (1 Cor 9:16–23)

The harvest here is indeed great, and the laborers
are few and imperfectly fitted, without much grace,
for such a work. And yet grace can make a few feeble
instruments the means of accomplishing great
things—things greater even than we can conceive.

J. Hudson Taylor (EMQ4)

❖   ❖   ❖

We must not over-focus on technique, or clever
approaches. We dare not say we will accomplish this
task because we have the money and the technology.
It will be accomplished only because of the greatness
of the gospel, the lordship of Christ, and the
glory of God in the face of Christ, with authentic,
transformed, joyful lives.

Lindsay Brown (LB)

❖   ❖   ❖

"But you will receive power when the Holy Spirit
has come upon you, and you will be my witnesses in
Jerusalem and in all Judea and Samaria, and to the
end of the earth."

Jesus (Acts 1:8)

We must not be contented however with praying, without exerting ourselves in the use of means for the obtaining of those things we pray for. Were the children of light but as wise in their generation as the children of this world they would stretch every nerve to gain so glorious a prize, nor ever imagine that it was to be obtained in any other way.

William Carey (PWCM, 299)

❖ ❖ ❖

Good spiritual logistics demand that we use every means available to us today to reach a lost world that desperately needs Christ.

Clarence W. Jones (QAM)

❖ ❖ ❖

The use of means ought not to lessen our faith in GOD; and our faith in GOD ought not to hinder our using whatever means He has given us for the accomplishment of His own purposes.

J. Hudson Taylor (JHTR, 41)

MESSAGE OF MISSIONS

The person who doesn't believe in taking the message of Jesus Christ to the nations, in the end, does not believe in Jesus Christ. No interest in missions means no interest for that particular thing for which Jesus was content to be born and to live and to die.

———

An address from the Student Volunteer Movement Convention, 1898 (ITG, 248)

❖　❖　❖

Witnesses must be faithful not only to the bare facts of the Christ-event, but also to their meaning. That is, modern witnesses are summoned to speak of the life, death and resurrection of Christ in such a way that the intrinsic divine significance of these events is brought to light.

———

Allison A. Trites (ETM, 42)

According to religious pluralism, truth is not *disclosed* to us but *discovered* by us through our experience. The writings of the different religions are thought to be different discoveries—through human experience—of the one God. And since the different religions are taken to be different expressions of the Absolute, each is believed to contain facets of the truth. More careful students of religion, however, recognize that different religions move on different axes. In truth, the similarities between Christianity and other religions are in peripheral things, not in the essentials of the faith. It is simply not correct to say that they teach essentially the same thing.

Ajith Fernando (PWCM, 169)

❖ ❖ ❖

In this the love of God was made manifest among us, that God sent his only Son into the world, so that we might live through him. In this is love, not that we have loved God but that he loved us and sent his Son to be the propitiation for our sins.

Apostle John (1 John 4:9–10)

153

While the missionary has none of the outward accouterments usually associated with diplomatic protocol, nevertheless his credentials are impeccable. He is the bearer of a divine revelation enshrined in an infallible Book. He has the law of God in his mouth, the rod of God in his hand, and the power of God in his life. His message, given to him by his Sovereign, he delivers without fear, favor, or flattery. The message itself is both clear and simple.

J. Herbert Kane (UCM, 31–32)

❖ ❖ ❖

The pastor needs to study three things: the world in its sin and misery, Christ in His dying love, and the Church as the link between the two. The minister must study it, so he will learn to preach in new power—missions, the great work, the supreme end, of Christ, of the Church, of every congregation, of every believer, and especially of every minister.

Andrew Murray (AM, 109)

For I am not ashamed of the gospel, for it is the power of God for salvation to everyone who believes, to the Jew first and also to the Greek. For in it the righteousness of God is revealed from faith for faith, as it is written, "The righteous shall live by faith."

Apostle Paul (Rom 1:16–17)

❖ ❖ ❖

True repentance has intellectual, emotional and volitional elements. Intellectually, it involves a change of mind about God, sin, Christ and oneself. The resultant change of mind views God as good and holy; sin as evil and injurious before God and people; Christ as perfect, necessary, and sufficient for salvation; and oneself as guilty and in need of salvation. Such repentance is an essential element of missionary proclamation.

Bill Thrasher (EDWM, 824)

❖ ❖ ❖

Like cold water to a thirsty soul, so is good news from a far country.

King Solomon (Prov 25:25)

The God of the Bible is the God of justice and of justification. The Christian evangelist has a message doubly relevant to the modern scene: he knows that justice is due to all because a just God created mankind in his holy image, and he knows that all men need justification because the Holy Creator sees us as rebellious sinners.

Carl F. H. Henry (WWP)

❖ ❖ ❖

Four words describe Christianity: Admit, Submit, Commit, Transmit.

Bishop Samuel Wilberforce (DCQ)

❖ ❖ ❖

The Gospel is good news not simply because it reinforces modern man's lost sense of personal worth and confirms the demand for universal justice on the basis of creation, but also because it offers rebellious men as doomed sinners that justification and redemption without which no man can see God.

Carl F. H. Henry (B66)

156

That's our message. Because Christ has died, He
has absorbed the wrath of God. He has canceled
sin. Everyone who is united to him by faith alone is
forgiven of their sins and counted righteous in Christ
and has eternal life. "Come, O nations. Come to
Christ!" That is our message.

John Piper (JP1)

❖ ❖ ❖

The gospel is only good news if it gets there in time.

Carl F. H. Henry (SNU)

❖ ❖ ❖

As the gospel is preached and the message is accepted,
the first fruit of mission is reconciliation with
God. One of the greatest strivings of the manifold
religions of humanity is to find peace with God,
the gods, or the unseen powers. Sacrificial systems,
ritual washings, pilgrimages, ascetic practices, and
cultic rites are all used in attempts to attain this. For
others life has lost significance because there is no
significant relationship to the source of all meaning,
the living God.

Craig Ott (ETM, 96)

The Christian faith ... is absolutely unique. There is no faith like it. No other god; no other Christ; no other Calvary; no other empty tomb; no other redemption; no other salvation; no other heaven.

David Hesselgrave (ENRM, 149)

❖ ❖ ❖

The Gospel is not an old, old story, freshly told. It is a fire in the Spirit, fed by the flame of Immortal Love; and woe unto us, if through our negligence to stir up the Gift of God which is within us, that fire burns low.

Dr. R. Moffat Gautrey (HM)

❖ ❖ ❖

For by grace you have been saved through faith. And this is not your own doing; it is the gift of God, not a result of works, so that no one may boast. For we are his workmanship, created in Christ Jesus for good works, which God prepared beforehand, that we should walk in them.

Apostle Paul (Eph 2:8–10)

Echoing from Creation to Calvary to Consummation, God's eternal Word invites a parched humanity to the well that never runs dry, to the Water of Life that alone truly and fully quenches the thirst of stricken pilgrims.

Carl F. H. Henry (CH1, 114)

❖ ❖ ❖ •

If God's love is for anybody anywhere, it's for everybody everywhere.

Edward Lawlor, Nazarene General Superintendent (SNU)

❖ ❖ ❖

The primary problem is not that people are unhappy. … The disease from which men and women suffer is that they are under the judgment and wrath of a holy God and need to be put right with him. It remains as true today as it was in Peter's day that however people may dislike it, forgiveness is their primary need and the gospel's primary offer.

Eric J. Alexander (EJA)

Turn to me and be saved,
all the ends of the earth!
For I am God, and there is no other.
By myself I have sworn;
from my mouth has gone out in righteousness
word that shall not return:
To me every knee shall bow,
every tongue shall swear allegiance.

Prophet Isaiah (Isa 45:22–23)

❖   ❖   ❖

So, is caring for others "the gospel"? Is that
evangelism? No, not without the spoken message of
the gospel of Jesus. The gospel message is the message
that produces salvation. So, we should never confuse
meeting physical needs with sharing the gospel.
Caring for others represents the gospel, it upholds
the gospel, it points to the gospel, it's an implication
of the gospel, but it is not the gospel, and it is not
equal to the gospel.

J. Mack Stiles (MOM, 68–69)

160

I am sending you to open their eyes, so that they may turn from darkness to light and from the power of Satan to God, that they may receive forgiveness of sins and a place among those who are sanctified by faith in me.

Jesus (Acts 26:17–18)

✦ ✦ ✦

Then he said to them, "These are my words that I spoke to you while I was still with you, that everything written about me in the Law of Moses and the Prophets and the Psalms must be fulfilled." Then he opened their minds to understand the Scriptures, and said to them, "Thus it is written, that the Christ should suffer and on the third day rise from the dead, and that repentance and forgiveness of sins should be proclaimed in his name to all nations, beginning from Jerusalem. You are witnesses of these things. And behold, I am sending the promise of my Father upon you. But stay in the city until you are clothed with power from on high."

Jesus (Luke 24:44–49)

Christ did not have to die merely because I am a sinner. He had to die because God in his infinite holiness and justice is angry at the world. We are children of anger. We are justly deserving of the wrath and the anger of God. This is the greatest problem for mankind in the universe. There isn't anything that surpasses lostness and being bound for an everlasting suffering under the wrath of God.

John Piper (JP1)

❖ ❖ ❖

In Christ, we become new creatures. His life becomes ours. Take that word "life" and turn it over and over and press it and try to measure it, and see what it will yield. Eternal life is a magnificent idea which comprises everything the heart can yearn after. Do not your hearts yearn for this life, this blessed and eternal life, which the Son of God so freely offers?

Mary Slessor (WW)

"You are my witnesses," declares the Lord,
"and my servant whom I have chosen,
that you may know and believe me
and understand that I am he.
Before me no god was formed,
nor shall there be any after me.
I, I am the Lord,
and besides me there is no savior.
I declared and saved and proclaimed,
when there was no strange god among you;
and you are my witnesses," declares the Lord.

Prophet Isaiah (Isa 43:10–12)

❖　❖　❖

We do not truly understand the gospel if we spend all
of our time preaching it to Christians.
The gospel is a missionary gospel.
It is a communication of Good News to people and
in places where the name of Christ is unknown.

David Sitton (TET)

We are called to proclaim the good news of Christ's
life-giving victory over the sinful separation from
God that disfigures human character, blinds people
to truth and leaves them without reliable power to
overcome the brokenness of creation, the darkness
of death, and the limits of human love. This gospel is
God's wonderful invitation to be saved from sin for a
beautiful new life through him.

Daniel Meyer (WE, 36)

❖ ❖ ❖

The Gospel is not how people get to heaven.
The Gospel is how people get to God.

John Piper (JP3)

❖ ❖ ❖

Cheap grace is the preaching of forgiveness without
requiring repentance—communion without
confession, absolution without personal confession.
Cheap grace is grace without discipleship, grace
without the cross, grace without Jesus Christ, living
and incarnate.

Dietrich Bonhoeffer (TCOD, 47)

METHODOLOGY

It would have been impossible for one in foreign dress to go to places to which I had to go if I were ever to discover the truth about things in India.

Amy Carmichael (TFS, 39–40)

❖ ❖ ❖

I believe we have been romantic in our view of working ourselves out of a job in the area of training and teaching the nationals and that this has been our detriment in the historic mission fields. I believe in the principles of self-governing, self-sustaining, and self-propagating; however, this is more for the local church and not as cleanly applicable to a nation, a people group, and an association of churches that need specialized assistance in teaching and theological education.

David Bledsoe (R&T, 74)

Those who would be employed in propagating the
Gospel should be familiar with the doctrines he is to
combat and the doctrines he is to teach, and acquire a
complete knowledge both of the Sacred Scriptures, and
of these philosophical and mythological dogmas which
form the souls of the Buddhist and Hindoo Systems.

William Carey (WCM, 292)

❖ ❖ ❖

We must begin with positive teaching, not with negative
prohibitions, and be content to wait and to watch
whilst the native Christians slowly recreate their own
customs as the Spirit of Christ gradually teaches them.

Roland Allen (SEC, 79)

❖ ❖ ❖

All authority in heaven and on earth has been given
to me. Go therefore and make disciples of all nations,
baptizing them in the name of the Father and of the
Son and of the Holy Spirit, teaching them to observe
all that I have commanded you. And behold, I am
with you always, to the end of the age.

Jesus (Matt 28:18–20)

MISSION OF MISSIONS

When a house is burning in the dead of night, the first and great concern is not for the house, but for the sleeping dwellers therein. Similarly the missionary's first and great concern is for the soul, to save it from impending wrath. In due time when men and women are truly reconciled to God, a social renovation will be sure to follow. Such an approach to missionary activity remains the good old way, marked with the footsteps of the apostles that brings peace with God and peace with one another.

American Board of Commissioners for Foreign Missions,
1812 (TMTH)

The essence of the task to be carried out by God's "messenger-missionaries" is to employ Scripture to the salvation of sinners, the formation of the church, the defense of truth, and the unmasking of error. That is what makes missionaries (and pastors and all of "God's messengers" for that matter) competent and that is what equips them and those who hear them to do "every good work" as well as to share every good "word" (2 Thess 2:17).

David J. Hesselgrave (MGSB, 1277)

The Great Commission is the mission of the church. Or to put it a bit longer: *the mission of the church is to go into the world and make disciples by declaring the gospel of Jesus Christ in the power of the Spirit and gathering these disciples into churches, that they might worship and obey Jesus Christ now and in eternity to the glory of God the Father ...* mission is not everything God is doing in the world, nor the social transformation of the world or our societies, nor everything we do in obedience to Christ.

Kevin Deyong and Greg Gilbert (WMC, 241)

The third millennium may bring us back to a situation reminiscent of the early church, where our mission will necessarily be from weakness, foolishness, and poverty.

Charles Van Engen (TGC, 202)

❖ ❖ ❖

It is impossible to come up with a scientific definition of the term "missionary" that will meet all the conditions and satisfy all the demands. It is possible to punch holes in any definition on which we might settle. In the traditional sense the term "missionary" has been reserved for those who have been called by God to a full-time ministry of the Word and prayer (Acts 6:4), and who have crossed geographical and/or cultural boundaries (Acts 22:21) to preach the gospel in those areas of the world where Jesus Christ is largely, if not entirely, unknown (Rom 15:20). This definition, though by no means perfect, has the virtue of being Biblical.

J. Herbert Kane (UCM, 28)

In the end, the Great Commission must be the mission of the church for two very basic reasons: there is something worse than death, and there is something better than human flourishing.

Kevin Deyong and Greg Gilbert (WMC, 242)

❖　❖　❖

Christianity is in its very essence a mission to the world. If it is not reaching, teaching, baptizing, and multiplying disciples, it is not Christianity.

Michael Horton (MH, 87)

❖　❖　❖

When the gospel takes root in our souls, it impels us outward to the alleviation of all unjust human suffering ... when the gospel takes root in our souls, it awakens us to the horrible reality of eternal suffering in hell under the wrath of a just God. And it impels us out to rescue the perishing.

John Piper (JP1)

MISSION OF MISSIONS

Missions is primarily intentional cross-cultural
evangelism beyond the immediate outreach of the
local church. Its aim is to bring the unreached to
saving faith in Jesus Christ, to disciple them and to
incorporate them into the fellowship of an existing
or newly planted local assembly of believers. Adjunct
ministries, to be considered "missions" should
demonstrate their commitment to evangelism,
discipleship and church planting/church growth.

Dr. Frank Allen, Highland Park Baptist Church,
Southfield, MI (FQC)

❖ ❖ ❖

Thus the mission of the church is not only that of
employing the keys of the Kingdom to open to both
Jew and Gentile the door into the eternal life which is
the gift of God's Kingdom; it is also the instrument
of God's dynamic rule in the world to oppose evil
and the powers of Satan in every form of their
manifestation.

George Eldon Ladd (ETM, 87)

Although proclamation alone cannot be seen as
an adequate definition of the missionary task, it
certainly is the necessary starting point of mission.
The explicit statements of the Great Commission,
the example of the apostles, and the logic of the
gospel make proclamation fundamental. Mission
that does not explicitly bring the good news of God's
salvation in Jesus Christ to the world cannot be
considered biblical mission.

Craig Ott (ETM, 113)

❖   ❖   ❖

I have been given say over everything on heaven
and earth. So go make apprentices to me among
people of every kind. Submerge them in the reality
of the Trinitarian God. And lead them into doing
everything I have told you to do. Now look! I am with
you every minute, until the job is completely done!

Dallas Willard (paraphrase of Matt 28:18–20)

❖   ❖   ❖

Mission is the intentional crossing of barriers from
Church to non-church in word and deed for the sake
of the proclamation of the Gospel.

Stephen Neill (SN)

As followers of Christ we have a treasure in God and His Kingdom (Matt 13:44). The good news is that this treasure is not limited to certain places or people—it is for all peoples—from every language, people group and nation. It is our joy to communicate the unsurpassed value of this treasure by serving the needs of others through our lives, professions, skills and words! As we do so we are privileged to see churches established among peoples who have never had one in their own language, culture or proximity.

Steve Coffey, president, Christar (SC)

❖ ❖ ❖

If everything is mission, nothing is mission. If everything the church does is to be classed as "mission," we shall need to find another term for the church's particular responsibility for "the heathen," those who have never yet heard the Name of Christ.

Stephen Neill (ETM, 79)

MOBILIZATION

I am more and more convinced that the question
of the right selection and training of missionaries
is beyond all comparison the major question in
the whole missionary enterprise. The really critical
period in a missionary's career is his first term of
service. ... A great deal of the instruction given before
he sails is lost to him because he cannot relate it to
anything in his life.

Dr. J. H. Oldham (IFMA, 396)

❖ ❖ ❖

He who does the work is not so profitably employed
as he who multiplies the doers.

John R. Mott (MF2)

Mobilizers and missionaries have two very different
kinds of jobs, both of them essential—equally
essential—to the World Christian Movement.
Many people unthinkingly equate "missions" with
missionaries. But there would be few missionaries
unless there were also intensely committed and skilled
mobilizers.

Ralph Winter (RDW, 377–378)

❖ ❖ ❖

Bear in mind that most mission agencies are doing
their very best (in the selection of missionaries) and it
is a difficult task to sort out the candidates who apply.
David Hesselgrave reminds us, "Availability and
suitability are both essential elements of a 'missionary
call.' The monumental challenge is to identify who
are both available and suitable for service."

David Sills (TMC, 71)

❖ ❖ ❖

Some of us are senders and some are goers.
Neither is more important than the other.
Neither is possible without the other.

David Sills (TMC)

A soft-drink company in Atlanta has done a better job getting brown sugar water to these people than the church of Jesus Christ has done in getting the gospel to them.

David Platt (RAD, 159)

❖ ❖ ❖

No new cross-cultural mission thrust comes apart from a season of renewal where the depth of abandoned devotion to Jesus Christ is increased among the people of God. It is only from this motive of deepened love and obedience to follow Jesus Christ that new cross-cultural mission thrusts break through and produce fruit that remains.

Ryan Shaw (SVM2)

MOTIVATION

The motive is this, "Oh, that God could be glorified, that Jesus might see the reward of his sufferings! Oh, that sinners might be saved, so that God might have new tongues to praise him, new hearts to love him! Oh, that sin were put an end to, that the holiness, righteousness, mercy, and power of God might be magnified!" This is the way to pray; when thy prayers seek God's glory, it is God's glory to answer thy prayers.

——

Charles Spurgeon (HM)

❖ ❖ ❖

The will of God—nothing less, nothing more, nothing else.

——

F. E. Marsh (SMU)

The message of John 3:16 is the reason for the Great Commission. If it did not exist, neither would the Great Commission. There would be no need for it. There would be no need to go anywhere. There would be no need to make disciples. There would be no need to baptize, teach or plant churches. There would be no need to make sacrifices for Jesus, because Jesus would not have sacrificed for us. But we know the opposite to be true. The truth of John 3:16 is a reality that happened. It is the reason for the Great Commission.

———

M. Newell (MJN, 126)

❖ ❖ ❖

The motivation for missionary work should flow out of our understandings of the purpose, nature, and task of mission. But knowing *what* we should do is not the same as understanding *why* we do it. Though we may have clarified the *reason* for mission, this may not be enough to move the *will* to undertake mission. Motivation influences the *spirit* and the *commitment* with which missionary work is conducted. Motivation reflects attitudes, and attitudes in turn impact relationships and methods in profound ways.

———

Craig Ott (ETM, 165)

All my desire was the conversion of the heathen. ...
I cared not where or how I lived, or what hardships I
went through, so that I could but gain souls to Christ.
I declare, now I am dying, I would not have spent my
life otherwise for the whole world.

David Brainerd, age 29 (BSWE)

❖ ❖ ❖

Missions is not only the most urgent task facing
believers; it is also each believer's greatest joy and
privilege. Even as heaven rejoices when one lost
person comes to Christ (Luke 15:7,10,32), we can
share the joy of God himself by sharing the good news
with people around us. We each can have the privilege
of carrying the transforming message of the gospel
to people in need of rescue. Though there are many
motivations for missions, we must never forget that
people are lost apart from God's grace, and the New
Testament pattern for receiving God's grace is clearly
the proclaimed message of the cross of Christ. Those
who accept the message will be forever grateful that
someone cared enough to carry the message to them;
that messenger's coming will always be beautiful.

Stephen Strauss (ETM, 338)

You can give without loving. But you cannot love without giving.

Amy Carmichael (GMN)

❖ ❖ ❖

We must shatter the notion that our main motivation for global mission is generated by pity for those who have less than we do. The main motivation for global mission should be that God deserves the worship of all people everywhere, and that we have been called to take the good news to those who are under the power of the enemy, whether they live in mud huts or in fine brick homes with a Mercedes-Benz in the garage.

Charlie Davis (CD)

❖ ❖ ❖

Life is precarious, and life is precious. Don't presume you will have it tomorrow, and don't waste it today.

John Piper (JP2)

"Not called!" did you say? "Not heard the call," I think you should say. Put your ear down to the Bible, and hear Him bid you go and pull sinners out of the fire of sin. Put your ear down to the burdened, agonized heart of humanity, and listen to its pitiful wail for help. Go stand by the gates of hell, and hear the damned entreat you to go to their father's house and bid their brothers and sisters and servants and masters not to come there. Then look Christ in the face—whose mercy you have professed to obey—and tell Him whether you will join heart and soul and body and circumstances in the march to publish His mercy to the world.

William Booth (DCQ)

❖ ❖ ❖

For a long time I felt much depressed after preaching the unsearchable riches of Christ to apparently insensible hearts; but now I like to dwell on the love of the great Mediator, for it always warms my heart, and I know that the gospel is the power of God—the great means which he employs for the regeneration of our ruined world.

David Livingstone (EMQ4)

The concern for world evangelization is not something tacked on to a man's personal Christianity, which he may take or leave as he chooses. It is rooted in the character of the God who has come to us in Christ Jesus. Thus, it can never be the province of a few enthusiasts, a sideline or a specialty of those who happen to have a bent that way. It is the distinctive mark of being a Christian.

James S. Stewart (BSWE)

❖ ❖ ❖

The infinite, all-glorious Creator of the universe, by whom and for whom all things exist—who holds every person's life in being at every moment (Acts 17:25)—is disregarded, disbelieved, disobeyed, and dishonored among the peoples of the world. That is the ultimate reason for missions.

John Piper (LNBG, 206)

❖ ❖ ❖

No one has the right to hear the gospel twice, while there remains someone who has not heard it once.

Oswald J. Smith (GMN)

How many there are … who imagine that because
Jesus paid it all, they need pay nothing, forgetting
that the prime object of their salvation was that they
should follow in the footsteps of Jesus Christ in
bringing back a lost world to God.

———

Lottie Moon (IMB)

❖ ❖ ❖

If God's loving invitation to eternal life does not
motivate us to share the good news with people,
what about the bad news? What about warning people
to flee from the wrath to come? We would do well
to soberly confront people with the reality (in C. S.
Lewis's terms) that they can choose to follow Jesus
and say, "Thy will be done," or they can choose to
reject Jesus, who as the Judge will say to them,
"Thy will be done," releasing them to their
destination of choice, the fires of hell.

———

Paul Borthwick (PB, 81)

❖ ❖ ❖

Sympathy is no substitute for action.

———

David Livingstone (SMU)

The true scandal of mission is not that evangelicals believe that Jesus is the only way of salvation but that many who claim to believe this are doing little or nothing to spread the gospel to lost people around the world. Paul's passion to preach the gospel controlled his life (Rom 9:1–4; 10:1; 15:18–21). If we have no reason to believe that any individual will spend eternity with God unless that person puts his or her faith in Christ, then mission becomes the most urgent task of the church and of every individual believer.

Stephen Strauss (ETM, 338)

MOTIVATION

If God desires every knee to bow to Jesus and every
tongue to confess him, so should we. We should
be "jealous" (as Scripture sometimes puts it) for
the honour of his name—troubled when it remains
unknown, hurt when it is ignored, indignant
when it is blasphemed, and all the time anxious
and determined that it shall be given the honour
and glory which are due to it. The highest of all
missionary motives is neither obedience to the Great
Commission (important as that is), nor love for
sinners who are alienated and perishing (strong as
that incentive is, especially when we contemplate
the wrath of God), but rather zeal-burning and
passionate zeal—for the glory of Jesus Christ. ...
Before this supreme goal of the Christian mission,
all unworthy motives wither and die.

John R. W. Stott (MGP, 246)

OBEDIENCE

The Christian is not obedient unless he is doing all in his power to send the Gospel to the heathen world.

———

A. B. Simpson (SNU)

❖ ❖ ❖

Obedience to God's will is the secret of spiritual knowledge and insight. It is not willingness to know, but willingness to DO God's will that brings certainty.

———

Eric Liddell (TGE, 12)

❖ ❖ ❖

It is not enough to do God's work; it must be done in His way and for His credit.

———

Erwin Lutzer (EL)

The command has been to "go," but we have stayed—
in body, gifts, prayer and influence. He has asked us
to be witnesses unto the uttermost parts of the earth
… but 99 percent of Christians have kept puttering
around in the homeland.

Robert Savage (TTT)

There is something essentially obscene about
arrogance in Christian people and something
essentially authentic about humility. We shall
not be able to strut round heaven like peacocks,
flattering ourselves as if we have got there by our
own achievement. Instead, we shall spend eternity
ascribing salvation to God and to the Lamb.

John R. W. Stott (JS3)

It is not in our choice to spread the gospel or not.
It is our death if we do not.

Peter Taylor Forsyth (SNU)

We are not engaged in an enterprise of our own choosing or devising. We are invited to participate in an activity of God which is the central meaning of creation itself. We are invited to become, through the presence of the Holy Spirit, participants in the Son's loving obedience to the Father.

Lesslie Newbigin (ETM, 75)

❖　❖　❖

Missions, in this large sense, is the response of Christian obedience to the explicit command of the risen Lord, "Go ye into all the world and preach the gospel to every creature." That order has never been countermanded; it determines forever the nature and the measure of the obligation of the Church. We have no right to hesitate in obeying it. True obedience will not go picking and choosing its way among the commandments of the Lord.

Report of the Toronto Convention 1902 (WWE, 108)

❖　❖　❖

Prepare for the worst; expect the best, and take what comes.

Robert E. Speer (EMQ3)

God isn't looking for people of great faith, but for individuals ready to follow Him.

J. Hudson Taylor (TMQ)

❖ ❖ ❖

No generation of Christians has been fully obedient to Christ's Great Commission. And yet, no generation of human beings can be reached except by the Christians of that generation. For sixty generations of lost people it is too late. And yet, according to the promise of God, some generation will be able to stand before the Lord and say, "It is finished. The task you have given us to do, we have accomplished."

Robertson McQuilkin (TGO, 79)

❖ ❖ ❖

Go, send, or disobey.

John Piper (SNU)

Is not the commission of our Lord still binding upon us? Can we not do more than now we are doing?

William Carey (SNU)

❖ ❖ ❖

I have a holy awe of the Lord. In a certain sense I am afraid of Him, for when God gives a command He means business; there is no foolishness with Him, and if the plea of love is not sufficient to elicit our obedience, then the Lord has His own methods of dealing with us. He is most gloriously a God of love, but it is a terrible thing to oppose the Ruler of the universe. The fear of the Lord is the beginning of wisdom, and I want to graduate from life's school with honors.

Robert Savage (LSM, 14)

OPPOSITION
(PERSECUTION)

Do not be surprised if there is an attack on your
work, on you who are called to do it, on your
innermost nature—the hidden person of the heart.
The great thing is not to be surprised, nor to count it
strange—for that plays into the hand of the enemy. Is
it possible that anyone should set himself to exalt our
beloved Lord and not instantly become a target for
many arrows?

Amy Carmichael (BTH)

❖ ❖ ❖

There is no neutral ground in the universe. Every
square inch, every split second, is claimed by God
and counterclaimed by Satan.

C. S. Lewis (LIR)

Circumstances may appear to wreck our lives and God's plans, but God is not helpless among the ruins. Our broken lives are not lost or useless. God's love is still working. He comes in and takes calamity and uses it victoriously, working out his wonderful plan for love.

Eric Liddell (BSWE)

❖ ❖ ❖

I know enough about Satan to realize that he will have all his weapons ready for determined opposition. He would be a missionary simpleton who expected plain sailing in any work of God.

James O. Fraser (TET)

❖ ❖ ❖

There are grave difficulties on every hand, and more are looming ahead—therefore, we must go forward.

William Carey (TET)

PARTNERSHIP

As disciples of Jesus, we are gospel people. The core of our identity is our passion for the biblical good news of the saving work of God through Jesus Christ. We are united by our experience of the grace of God in the gospel and by our motivation to make that gospel of grace known to the ends of the earth by every possible means.

(Capetown Commitment, CTC, 23)

❖ ❖ ❖

Real partnership is costly. We need to be willing to empower others to godly leadership and make their dreams possible, even at the expense of putting aside our own desires.

David Ruiz (DR)

For us in the Pacific, in Asia, in India, and in
Africa, Christian unity is not an optional extra. It
is an urgent necessity, for our divisions are a real
stumbling block to the proclamation of the Gospel.
… Mission is at the heart of the divine reality. It is
the will of God and the Kingdom of God which are
to be made known. Wherever we are, our purpose is
not to propagate the Church as an end in itself, but
to proclaim Christ as Lord of all life and as Savior
of all men.

John C. Vockler (JCV)

❖ ❖ ❖

Africans picture a partnership as a long-term
relationship using metaphors like marriage or
brothers. Expatriates usually see partnerships
like business arrangements with memoranda of
understanding and time limits. We may use family
terms but contract forms. Both partners may
become confused when they work from the familiar
family mentality but we are expecting to operate in a
contractual mode.

Mary Lederleitner (CCP, 40)

194

The foundation of all Christian partnerships is reconciliation. People who were once enemies because of political or racial conflicts, can now work shoulder-to-shoulder to proclaim the message of reconciliation. This message is to be lived out by God's new community, and the fragmented world needs to see it.

Patrick Fung (PF1)

❖ ❖ ❖

Therefore, since we are surrounded by so great a cloud of witnesses, let us also lay aside every weight, and sin which clings so closely, and let us run with endurance the race that is set before us, looking to Jesus, the founder and perfecter of our faith, who for the joy that was set before him endured the cross, despising the shame, and is seated at the right hand of the throne of God. Consider him who endured from sinners such hostility against himself, so that you may not grow weary or fainthearted.

Unknown (Heb 12:1–3)

Majority World partners are utterly amazed and confused that Western leaders will make a huge fuss over getting detailed accounting records for $5,000 sent abroad, all the while they seem to waste so much money in their own countries on things that do not seem wise or fruitful for the kingdom of God. Massive building programs frequently fall in this category. ... These extravagant buildings are insanity from a Third World perspective.

Mary Lederleitner (CCP, 54)

❖ ❖ ❖

The church in North America needs the ministry of Christians from India, Congo, or Brazil as much as the people in those countries require the services of Christians from North America.

Byang H. Kato (BHK)

❖ ❖ ❖

Community without mission dies out, and mission without community burns out.

Titus Presler (GGWG)

196

We are God's global community united in Christ.
Partnership is based upon this firm foundation.
Partnership must spring from a deep sense of
gratitude to God for what Christ has done. He has
destroyed the barrier, the dividing wall of hostility
that separates us from God and from one another.
Sacrificial partnership with a commitment to "death
to self" will be the only way to world evangelization,
for the very shape of mission is cruciform. The cross
lies at the very heart of mission.

———

Patrick Fung (PF1)

❖ ❖ ❖

Dependency is a problem when we do not see
correctly and discern correctly. What is a need in one
place might not be a need in another. Often there
are local resources and ways to solve issues that are far
wiser and better than imported solutions. We need to
take time to examine these before we begin to import
outside funds to do what the community, church or
ministry can accomplish on its own.

———

Mary Lederleitner (CCP, 144)

PASSION

James Gilmour in Mongolia, David Livingstone
in Central Africa, Grenfell on the Congo, Keith-
Falconer in Arabia, Dr. Rijnhart and Miss Annie
Taylor in Tibet, Chalmers in New Guinea, Morrison
in China, Henry Martyn in Persia, and all the others
like them had this "inverted home-sickness," this
passion to call that country their home which was
most in need of the Gospel. In this passion all other
passions died; before this vision all other visions
faded; this call drowned all other voices. They were
the pioneers of the Kingdom, the forelopers of God,
eager to cross the border-marches and discover new
lands or win new empires.

Samuel M. Zwemer (SMZ)

The Moravians took their inspiration from Isaiah 53:10–12, making our Lord's suffering the spur to their activity: To win for the Lamb that was slain, the reward of His sufferings. … They counted the service of God the one thing to live for, and everything was made subservient to this.

Andrew Murray (AM, 34)

❖ ❖ ❖

God is calling us above all else to be the kind of people whose theme and passion is the supremacy of God in all of life. No one will be able to rise to the magnificence of the missionary cause who does not feel the magnificence of Christ. There will be no big world vision without a big God. There will be no passion to draw others into our worship where there is no passion for worship.

John Piper (LNBG, 43)

❖ ❖ ❖

All that I am I owe to Jesus Christ, revealed to me in his divine book. Without Christ, not one step; with Him, anywhere!

David Livingstone (IMG)

Our God and Father, who has delayed the day of judgment for the sake of those who are yet to be saved, we pray that all rulers may fear you, so that evil might be restrained in the world. Look down upon your servants, those who would be martyred were it not for the protection of the angels, and let them testify of your tender mercies and your love. At this hour, near the end of the age, we ask that the angels might gather their elect from the four corners of the earth, and that the coming day of judgment may seize men everywhere with terror. For the sake of pity we ask that you would wait longer still before drawing your sword. As many fled with the Hebrews from Egypt, on account of their faith expressed by putting the blood of the lamb on their doorposts, so now, O God, grant that those whom we would least expect to believe will turn to the living God and be saved, and prove themselves to be yours by their courage to restore righteousness, peace and joy on earth. This we pray in Jesus' name. Amen.

Bob Blincoe, U.S. Director of Frontiers (BB)

❖ ❖ ❖

No reserve. No retreat. No regrets.

William Borden (MJN, 110)

I have but one passion: It is He, it is He alone.
The world is the field and the field is the world;
and henceforth that country shall be my home where
I can be most used in winning souls for Christ.

Count Nicolaus Ludwig von Zinzendorf (TTT)

❖ ❖ ❖

Where passion for God is weak, zeal for missions
will be weak. Churches that are not centered on
the exaltation of the majesty and beauty of God will
scarcely kindle a fervent desire to "declare his glory
among the nations" (Ps 96:3).

John Piper (LNBG, 18)

❖ ❖ ❖

I hope you will be a missionary wherever your lot is
cast ... it makes but little difference after all where we
spend these few fleeting years, if they are only spent
for the glory of God. Be assured there is nothing else
worth living for.

Elizabeth Freeman (PGR, 128)

201

If I had a thousand pounds, China should have it.
If I had a thousand lives, China should have them.
No, not China, but Christ! Can we do too much
for Him?

J. Hudson Taylor (AJB1)

❖ ❖ ❖

I have but one candle of life to burn, and I would
rather burn it out in a land filled with darkness than
in a land flooded with light.

Ion Keith-Falconer (SNU)

❖ ❖ ❖

The highest form of worship is the worship of
unselfish Christian service. The greatest form of
praise is the sound of consecrated feet seeking out the
lost and helpless.

Billy Graham (QUO)

❖ ❖ ❖

Never pity missionaries; envy them. They are where
the real action is—where life and death, sin and grace,
Heaven and Hell converge.

Robert C. Shannon (GMN)

I believe there are two things sadly lacking among God's people today. One is that we do not sorrow ... people are borne down with grief because of the loss of loved ones, because of frustrations, or hurts of one kind or another that affect them personally; but they give very small proportion of their attention to the sorrow that stabs the heart of God, the grief that pierced the Saviour on the cross. They do not have deep concern for the millions of lost souls who are without Christ—at least not enough to drive them to hours of intercessory prayer or to count everything else of little importance in comparison to reaching them for Christ.

Joy Ridderhof (GRN2)

❖ ❖ ❖

As soon as we separate quality from the deepest passion of our Lord to seek and save the lost, it ceases to be Christian quality. ... Even if we produce Christians who live as full brothers with men of other races, but do not burn with the desire that those others may have eternal life, their "quality" is certainly in doubt.

Donald McGavran (UCG, 52)

Oh, that my words could be as a trumpet call
stirring the hearts of my brethren and sisters to
pray, to labor, to give themselves to this people!

Lottie Moon (STL, 83)

❖ ❖ ❖

As we have a high old time this Christmas may we
who know Christ hear the cry of the damned as they
hurtle headlong into the Christless night without ever
a chance. May we be moved with compassion as our
Lord was. May we shed tears of repentance for these
we have failed to bring out of darkness. Beyond the
smiling scenes of Bethlehem may we see the crushing
agony of Golgotha.

Nate Saint (SOM)

❖ ❖ ❖

Some wish to live within the sound of a chapel bell;
I wish to run a rescue mission within a yard of hell.

C. T. Studd (SNU)

Oh, that I had a thousand lives and a thousand
bodies! All of them should be devoted to no other
employment but to preach Christ to these degraded,
despised, yet beloved mortals.

Robert Moffat (BSWE)

❖　❖　❖

I am ready to burn out for God. I am ready to endure
any hardship, if by any means I might save some. The
longing of my heart is to make known my glorious
Redeemer to those who have never heard.

William Burns (BSWE)

❖　❖　❖

If there is no passionate love for Christ at the center
of everything, we will only jingle and jangle our way
across the world, merely making a noise as we go.

William Wilberforce (HM)

Perseverance
(Faithfulness)

A little thing is a little thing, but faithfulness in a little thing is a big thing.

J. Hudson Taylor (AJB, 154)

✧ ✧ ✧

If we are faithful to GOD in little things, we shall gain experience and strength that will be helpful to us in the more serious trials of life.

J. Hudson Taylor (JHT, 20)

✧ ✧ ✧

I can plod; I can persevere in any definite pursuit. To this I owe everything.

William Carey (GM, 225)

Therefore, my beloved brothers, be steadfast, immovable, always abounding in the work of the Lord, knowing that in the Lord your labor is not in vain.

Apostle Paul (1 Cor 15:58)

❖ ❖ ❖

Whatever can be said of my life and work, at least I have stayed put.

Robert E. Speer (MSG, 227)

❖ ❖ ❖

I am not tired of my work, neither am I tired of the world; yet, when Christ calls me home, I shall go with gladness.

Adoniram Judson (TMM, 38)

❖ ❖ ❖

All things are possible to him who believes; they are less difficult to him who hopes; they are more easy to him who loves; and still more easy to him who perseveres in the practice of these three virtues.

Brother Lawrence (TGC, 152)

PERSPECTIVE

Remember, when you see a missionary coming home broken in body and weary in soul, it isn't the privations or dangers or things he's done that leave a deep hurt; it's the things he couldn't do that break his heart.

Anonymous Missionary (TET)

What are we here for, to have a good time with Christians or to save sinners?

Malla Moe (TTT)

If I die here in Glasgow, I shall be eaten by worms;
if I can but live and die serving the Lord Jesus, it
will make no difference to me whether I am eaten
by cannibals or by worms; for in the Great Day my
resurrection body will arise as fair as yours in the
likeness of our risen Redeemer.

John G. Paton (TMC, 188)

❖ ❖ ❖

We want to bring a fresh challenge to "bear witness to
Jesus Christ and all his teaching, in every part of the
world—not only geographically, but in every sphere
of society, and in the realm of ideas," identifying and
responding to key issues. I love the words of Abraham
Kuyper, the Dutch theologian and prime minister:
"There is not one centimeter of human existence to
which Christ, who is Lord of all, does not point and
say, 'that is mine.'"

Lindsay Brown (LB)

❖ ❖ ❖

We are a bunch of nobodies trying to exalt Somebody.

Jim Elliot (TET)

"God loves me" is not the essence of biblical Christianity. ... "God loves me, so that I might make him—his ways, his salvation, his glory, and his greatness—known among all nations." ... We are not the end of the gospel; God is. ... We have received salvation so that his name will be proclaimed in all nations. God loves us for his sake in the world. To disconnect God's blessing from God's global purpose is to spiral downward into an unbiblical, self-saturated Christianity that misses the point of God's grace.

David Platt (RAD, 70–71)

POWER

An easygoing non-self-denying life will never be one of power.

J. Hudson Taylor (AJB2, 310)

❖ ❖ ❖

I am convinced that those churches which are strongest in sending and supporting missionaries average no more than two or three minutes a week in united prayer for the missionary enterprise. Is there any wonder that the church has experienced a massive power failure so that darkness envelopes the world for which we are to be lights? The connection with our source of power is so tenuous, so sporadic, that we flicker and often seem simply to blink out.

Robertson McQuilkin (TGO, 63)

The question for us, then, is whether we trust in his power. And the problem for us is that in our culture we are tempted at every turn to trust in our own power instead. The dangerous assumption we unknowingly accept in the American dream is that our greatest asset is our own ability. Even more important is the subtly fatal goal we will achieve ... to our own glory.

David Platt (RAD, 45–46)

❖   ❖   ❖

The church today has grown and has manifold resources unimaginable to the first Christians. Nevertheless, the thought is no less absurd that we should be able to advance the kingdom one millimeter apart from God's enabling power. Jesus appointed us as his disciples to go and bear much fruit that will remain (John 15:16), but he could not have stated the importance of our total dependence on him more clearly: "apart from me you can do nothing" (John 15:5b).

Craig Ott (ETM, 76)

212

God uses men who are weak and feeble enough to lean on him.

J. Hudson Taylor (SNU)

❖ ❖ ❖

Usually when God is going to do a great work, I have noticed that there is a time of great dearth. Nothing moves. Nothing happens. All seems so stagnant. These are golden opportunities for prayer. Our Lord needs prayer, and keeps things from happening to open space for Himself. And he is that satisfying portion we need—that food and drink is Himself.

Joy Ridderhof (MS, 153)

❖ ❖ ❖

We may, indeed, force men to be hypocrites, but no power on earth can force men to become Christians.

William Carey (MHMF, 57)

PRAYER

I'm convinced that we are living in what appears to be the most cruel period of history. More people suffer for Christ's name than in any other generation. As Christians who are not under such persecution, we must find any way that we can to help our persecuted brothers and sisters. They need us more than ever—our presence, our encouragement, our support, our teaching, our fellowship, and perhaps more than anything else, our prayers. Our prayers are crucial because our best praying will move us into our best action.

Brother Andrew (PWCM, 179)

❖ ❖ ❖

God answers all true prayers, either in kind or in kindness.

Adoniram Judson (CQ-AJ)

Prayer is the mighty engine that is to move the missionary work.

A. B. Simpson (HM)

❖ ❖ ❖

If you are sick, fast and pray; if the language is hard to learn, fast and pray; if the people will not hear you, fast and pray; if you have nothing to eat, fast and pray.

Frederick Franson (TTT)

❖ ❖ ❖

Do not have your concert first, and then tune your instrument afterwards. Begin the day with the Word of God and prayer, and get first of all into harmony with Him.

J. Hudson Taylor (DCQ-HT)

In our lifetime, wouldn't it be sad if we spent more time washing dishes or swatting flies or mowing the yard or watching television than praying for world missions?

Dave Davidson (EMT)

❖ ❖ ❖

The Bible is a promise book and a prayer book. And while reading is reactive, prayer is proactive. Reading is the way you get through the Bible; prayer is the way you get the Bible through you. As you pray, the Holy Spirit will quicken certain promises to your spirit. It's very difficult to predict what and when and where and how, but over time, the promises of God will become your promises. Then you need to circle those promises, both figuratively and literally.

Mark Batterson (TCM, Kindle location 1364)

❖ ❖ ❖

In no other way can the believer become as fully involved with God's work, especially the work of world evangelism, as in intercessory prayer.

Dick Eastman (FLI)

Christian missions is a supernatural venture. Only supernatural resources can sustain it and make it dynamic. The contact with the Divine is imperative. Prayer is not optional; it is operational and decisive.

George W. Peters (BTM, 345)

❖ ❖ ❖

Where are the men of prayer? Where are the men who, like Moses, commune with God face-to-face as a man speaks with his friend, and unmistakably bear with them the fragrance of that meeting through the day?

Howard Guinness (HG)

❖ ❖ ❖

Satan will always find you something to do when you ought to be occupied about that (prayer and Bible study)—if it is only arranging the window blind!

J. Hudson Taylor (TGE, 86)

Why are we so weak and impotent? Why have we watched in our lifetime as the number of lost people has increased geometrically? Are we not weak in impact for God because we are weak in time spent with God?

Robertson McQuilkin (TGO, 62)

❖ ❖ ❖

Bold prayers honor God, and God honors bold prayers. God isn't offended by your biggest dreams or boldest prayers. He is offended by anything less. If your prayers aren't impossible to you, they are insulting to God.

Mark Batterson (TCM, Kindle location 82)

❖ ❖ ❖

We can reach our world, if we will.
The greatest lack today is not people or funds.
The greatest need is prayer.

Wesley Duewel (TWTP, 13)

One of the primary reasons we don't pray through
is because we run out of things to say. Our lack of
persistence is really a lack of conversation pieces.
Like an awkward conversation, we don't know what to
say. Or like a conversation on its last leg, we run out
of things to talk about. That's when our prayers turn
into a bunch of overused and misapplied clichés.
So instead of praying hard about a big dream, we're
left with small talk. Our prayers are as meaningless
as a conversation about the weather. The solution?
Pray through the Bible. Prayer was never meant to be
a monologue; it was meant to be a dialogue. Think of
Scripture as God's part of the script;
prayer is our part. Scripture is God's way of initiating
a conversation; prayer is our response.

Mark Batterson (TCM, Kindle location 1355)

❖ ❖ ❖

Every step in the progress of missions is directly
traceable to prayer.

A. T. Pierson (TET)

To pray declares that God and his world are at cross-purposes; to "sleep," or "faint," or "lose heart" is to act as if they are not. Why, then, do we pray so little for our local church? Is it really that our technique is bad, our wills weak, or our imaginations listless? I don't believe so. There is plenty of strong-willed and lively discussion—which in part or in whole may be justified—about the mediocrity of the preaching, the emptiness of worship, the superficiality of the fellowship, and the ineffectiveness of the evangelism. So why, then, don't we pray as persistently as we talk? The answer, quite simply, is that we don't believe it will make any difference. We accept, however despairingly, that the situation is unchangeable, that what is will always be. This is not a problem about the practice of prayer, but rather about its *nature*. Or, more precisely, it is about the nature of God and his relationship with this world.

———

David Wells (PWCM, 144)

The amount of time I spend in prayer can indicate whether I am trusting in God or myself. Whatever else we do when support raising, we can't afford to neglect prayer. Only God can change hearts. We must talk to God about men before we talk to men about God. (When asking for significant end-of-the-year gifts, the author prayed for each person and asked God to lay a certain amount on that person's heart to give for that year.)

Steve Shadrach (SS, 17–18)

❖ ❖ ❖

When we depend upon our organizations, we get what organizations can do; when we depend upon education, we get what education can do; when we depend upon man, we get what man can do; but when we depend upon prayer, we get what God can do.

A. C. Dixon (ACD, 108)

❖ ❖ ❖

First, and most important: Go to your work directly from your knees. Do not leave your closet until you feel that God is with you, by his Spirit.

Sue McBeth (EMQ5, 147)

Prayers are prophecies. They are the best predictors of your spiritual future. Who you become is determined by how you pray. Ultimately, the transcript of your prayers becomes the script of your life.

Mark Batterson (TCM, Kindle location 97)

❖ ❖ ❖

This is going to sound sacrilegious, but sometimes you need to quit praying. After you pray through, you need to praise through. You need to quit asking God to do something and start praising Him for what He had already done. Prayer and praise are both expressions of faith, but praise is a higher dimension of faith. Prayer is asking God to do something, future tense; praise is believing that God has already done it, past tense.

Mark Batterson (TCM, Kindle location 480)

❖ ❖ ❖

Prayer is not getting man's will done in heaven, but getting God's will done on earth. It is not overcoming God's reluctance but laying hold of God's willingness.

Richard C. Trench (WBC, 1004)

We will only advance in our evangelistic work as fast and as far as we advance on our knees. Prayer opens the channel between a soul and God; prayerlessness closes it. Prayer releases the grip of Satan's power; prayerlessness increases it. That is why prayer is so exhausting and so vital. If we believed it, the prayer meeting would be as full as the church.

Alan Redpath (HM)

❖ ❖ ❖

If you are ever inclined to pray for a missionary, do it at once, wherever you are. Perhaps she may be in great peril at the moment. Once I had to deal with a crowd of warlike men in the compound, and I got strength to face them because I felt that someone was praying for me just then.

Mary Slessor (WQO, 113)

❖ ❖ ❖

Without prayer, even though there may be increased interest in missions, more work for them, better success in organization and greater finances, the real growth of the spiritual life and of the love of Christ in the people may be very small.

Andrew Murray (CRWM)

Prayer is a strategic weapon that is effective in cross-cultural evangelism. We can use it to impact situations and difficulties anywhere in the world, without leaving home. How much different the spiritual landscape would be if the Church would use this weapon more than it does. How much more light and less spiritual darkness there would be if we invested more time in intercessory prayer for the nations and unreached peoples of the world. Our paucity in prayer for missions has surely slowed the fulfilling of the Great Commission.

Colin Stott (GRN)

❖ ❖ ❖

We never know how God will answer our prayers, but we can expect that He will get us involved in His plan for the answer. If we are true intercessors, we must be ready to take part in God's work on behalf of the people for whom we pray.

Corrie Ten Boom (HM)

It will be good to fasten on reports of Christians
in several parts of the world ... and learn to
intercede with God on their behalf. Not only is this
an important expression of the fellowship of the
church, it is a critical discipline that will enlarge
our horizons, increase our ministry, and help us to
become world Christians.

D. A. Carson (DAC, 98)

❖ ❖ ❖

Just a word of warning. Passionate prayers not only
change the world, they have a way of transforming the
people who pray. ... God's goal is to recruit every one
of us for His search-and-rescue team.

Debbie Meroff (TG, viii)

❖ ❖ ❖

Almost everyone believes that prayer is important.
But there is a difference between believing that
prayer is important and believing it is essential.
"Essential" means there are things that will not
happen without prayer.

Dee Duke (HM)

To pray effectually, to pray till hell feels the stroke, to pray till the iron gates of difficulty are opened, till the mountains of obstacles are removed, till the mists are exhaled and the clouds lifted, is hard work; but it is God's work and man's best labor.

E. M. Bounds (EMB)

❖ ❖ ❖

No erudition, no purity of diction, no width of mental outlook, no flowers of eloquence, no grace of person can atone for lack of fire. Prayer ascends by fire. Flame gives prayer access as well as wings, acceptance as well as energy. There is no incense without fire; no prayer without flame.

E. M. Bounds (EMB)

❖ ❖ ❖

Prayer is the real work of the ministry.
Service is just gathering in the results of prayer.

S. D. Gordon (TTT)

We all have to wait until the astonishing discoveries
will one day be made, and find out whose faithful
prayer in hospitals, prisons, jungles, wheelchairs,
crowded city apartments, cabins in the woods, farms,
factories, or concentration camps has been a part of
a specific victory in snatching someone from a circle
of death, or in breaking chains so that there seems
to be an ease for that one in stepping into new life.
I feel sure that we'll be surprised beyond measure to
discover who or how many will receive the rewards for
their part in taking literally and with simple faith and
trust the responsibility to intercede, to pray, to make
requests day in and day out.

Edith Schaeffer (GGD)

❖ ❖ ❖

I used to think that prayer should have the first place
and teaching the second. I now feel it would be truer
to give prayer the first, second, and third places, and
teaching the fourth.

James O. Fraser (JOF)

227

Since the days of Pentecost, has the whole church ever put aside every other work and waited upon Him for ten days, that the Spirit's power might be manifested? We give too much attention to method and machinery and resources, and too little to the source of power.

J. Hudson Taylor (DCQ)

❖ ❖ ❖

The power of prayer has never been tried to its full capacity. If we want to see mighty wonders of the divine power and grace wrought in the place of weakness, failure, and disappointment, let us answer God's standing challenge, "Call unto me, and I will answer thee, and show thee great and mighty things which thou knowest not."

J. Hudson Taylor (TMQ)

❖ ❖ ❖

There is no alternative to prayer in a Christian worker's life. ... We simply cannot have a ministry that has spiritual depth, and therefore lasting effects, unless our lives are steeped in prayer.

Ajith Fernando (JDM, 223)

228

Why is prayer so critical for mission? Colossians 4:2–4 provides the answer. In prayer we lift the work of the gospel above mere circumstances and into the hands of the One who governs everything ... the One who can provide an "open door," even though the current messenger is locked up "in chains."

John Dickson (MGP, 257)

❖ ❖ ❖

This crucial place of prayer reaffirms that great goal of God to uphold and display his glory for the enjoyment of the redeemed from all the nations. ... The missionary purpose of God is as invincible as the fact that he is God. He will achieve his purpose by creating white-hot worshippers from every people, tongue, tribe and nation (Rev 5:9; 7:9). And he will be engaged to do it through prayer. Therefore, it is almost impossible to overemphasize the awesome place of prayer in the purposes of God for the world.

John Piper (MGP, 254)

If added power attends the united prayer of two
or three, what mighty triumphs there will be when
hundreds of thousands of consistent members of
the Church are with one accord day by day making
intercession for the extension of Christ's Kingdom.

John R. Mott (JRM, 189)

❖ ❖ ❖

Life is war. That is not all it is. But it is always
that. Our weakness in prayer is owing largely
to our neglect of this truth. Prayer is primarily
a wartime walkie-talkie for the mission of the
church as it advances against the powers of darkness
and unbelief. It is not surprising that prayer
malfunctions when we try to make it a domestic
intercom to call upstairs for more comforts. ...
Prayer gives us the significance of frontline forces,
and gives God the glory of a limitless provider.

John Piper (LNBG, 41)

❖ ❖ ❖

Prayer is not a preparation for the battle; it is the battle!

Leonard Ravenhill (HM)

Now here's the problem: Most of us don't get what
we want simply because we don't know what we want.
We've never circled any of God's promises. We've
never written down a list of life goals. We've never
defined success for ourselves. And our dreams are
as nebulous as cumulus clouds. Instead of drawing
circles, we draw blanks.

Mark Batterson (TCM, Kindle location 214)

❖ ❖ ❖

Praying without faith is like trying to cut with a blunt
knife—much labour expended to little purpose.

James O. Fraser (POF, 9)

❖ ❖ ❖

If we look through the whole Bible and observe all
the examples of prayer that we find there recorded,
we shall not find so many prayers for any other mercy
as for the deliverance, restoration and prosperity of
the church and the advancement of God's glory and
kingdom of grace in the world.

Jonathan Edwards (WJE, 291)

231

Prayer and missions are as inseparable as faith and works; in fact prayer and missions are faith and works. Jesus Christ, by precept, by command, and by example, has shown with great clearness and force that he recognizes the greatest need of the enterprise of worldwide evangelization to be prayer. Before "give" and before "go" comes "pray." This is the divine order. Anything that reverses or alters it inevitably leads to loss or disaster.

John R. Mott (ITG, 179–180)

❖ ❖ ❖

Much prayer, much power; little prayer, little power; no prayer, no power.

Peter Dyneka, founder, Slavic Gospel Association (SGA)

❖ ❖ ❖

I believe it will only be known on the Last Day how much has been accomplished in missionary work by the prayers of earnest believers at home. … I do earnestly covet a volume of prayer for my … work— but oh, for a volume of faith too! Will you give this?

James O. Fraser (JOF)

Do not pray for easy lives; pray to be stronger men.
Do not pray for tasks equal to your powers; pray for
powers equal to your tasks. Then the doing of your
work shall be no miracle, but you yourself shall be
a miracle. Every day you shall wonder at yourself,
at the richness of life which has come to you by the
grace of God.

Phillips Brooks (FQ-PB)

❖ ❖ ❖

Solid lasting missionary work is done on our knees.

James O. Fraser (JOF)

❖ ❖ ❖

We are too busy to pray, and so we are too busy to
have power. We have a great deal of activity, but we
accomplish little; many services but few conversions;
much machinery but few results.

R. A. Torrey (RAT, 81)

❖ ❖ ❖

Pray for great things, expect great things, work for
great things, but above all pray.

R. A. Torrey (HM)

The evangelization of the world depends first upon a revival of prayer. Deeper than the need for workers; deeper far than the need for money; deep down at the bottom of our spiritual lives, is the need for the forgotten secret of prevailing, worldwide prayer.

Robert E. Speer (BSWE)

❖   ❖   ❖

The history of missions is the history of answered prayer. It is the key to the whole mission problem. All human means are secondary.

Samuel M. Zwemer (TGE, 86)

❖   ❖   ❖

I have become convinced that the church will never complete God's purposes of redemption in the world in obedience to His great command unless God the Holy Spirit powerfully thrusts laborers into the harvest field. And we are commanded to participate in this sending out of workers first of all through prayer.

Robertson McQuilkin (TGO, 63)

PRIORITIES

The church is capable of doing any number of good things for the world. For example, it is a good thing to teach people to read and write, to provide clean water for people, to feed the hungry and clothe the naked, and care for God's earth. But the fact is the world can also do all of those good things and actually does them. Yet it is only the church that has been called by God to do what is best for the world since the world is incapable of doing that of itself, namely, preaching the gospel. Accordingly, we cannot afford to sacrifice what is best on the altar of what is good. Too much is at stake; indeed, the very eternal destiny of the lost is at stake.

Christopher Little (CL, 90)

Every saved soul is called to be a herald and a witness; and we are to aim at nothing less than this: to make every nation, and every creature in every nation, acquainted with God. This is the first and ever-present duty of the Church.

A. T. Pierson (MRW, 406)

❖ ❖ ❖

Christianity asserts that every individual human being is going to live forever, and this must be true or false. Now there are a good many things which would not be worth bothering about if I were going to live only seventy years, but which I had better bother about very seriously if I am going to live forever.

C. S. Lewis (CSL, 74)

❖ ❖ ❖

Here then we see God's way of success in our work—a trinity of prayer, faith and patience.

James O. Fraser (OMF1)

"Lo, I am with you always" (Matt 28:20). If we know
that Jesus is with us, every power will be developed,
and every grace will be strengthened, and we will cast
ourselves into the Lord's service with heart, soul,
and strength; therefore is the presence of Christ
to be desired above all things. His presence will be
more realized by those who are most like him. If you
desire to see Christ, you must grow in conformity to
him. Bring yourself, by the power of the Spirit, into
union with Christ's desires, and motives, and plans
of action, and you are likely to be favoured with his
company. Remember, his presence may be had.

Charles Spurgeon (MAE)

❖   ❖   ❖

The ultimate goal of Jesus for his disciples was that his
life be reproduced in them, and through them into
the lives of others.

Robert E. Coleman (MPE, 173)

God never told us to build magnificent cathedrals and invite the people to come in and hear us. God told us to send out the message. The message is dynamite. ... We make it a rule in The Peoples Church in Toronto that every time we invest one dollar in the home work in Toronto, we see to it that we send seven dollars to the regions beyond. That is why God blesses the work. I think that is the right proportion. Seven dollars for the foreign field, one dollar for ourselves at home.

Oswald J. Smith (FUT, 237)

❖ ❖ ❖

The mission was Paul's calling, but not his treasure. His treasure was God himself. Communion with God must be our highest priority.

Skye Jethani (NAMLC)

Let us feel that everything that is human, everything outside of the sufficiency of Christ, is only helpful in the measure in which it enables us to bring the soul to him. If our medical missions draw people to us, and we can present to them the Christ of God, medical missions are a blessing; but to substitute medicine for the preaching of the gospel would be a profound mistake. If we put schools or education in the place of spiritual power to change the heart, it will be a profound mistake. If we get the idea that people are going to be converted by some educational process, instead of by the regenerative re-creation, it will be a profound mistake. ... Let us exalt the glorious gospel in our hearts, and believe that it is the power of God unto salvation. Let everything else sit at its feet. ... We shall never be discouraged if we realize that in Christ is our sufficiency.

_____

J. Hudson Taylor (HT, chapter 28)

PROTECTION
(PROVIDENTIAL CARE)

The circumstance that had seemed a disaster was being recognized as among the "all things" that work together for good to them that love God ... learning to think of God as "The One Great Circumstance of Life" and of all lesser, eternal circumstances as the kindest ... wisest and best, because they were either ordered or permitted by him.

———

J. Hudson Taylor (HTSS)

❖ ❖ ❖

With God, anywhere; without him, not over the threshold.

———

John R. Mott (TGC, 138)

Matthew 28:18–20: This is the perpetual commission of the Church of Christ; and the great seal of the Kingdom attached to it, giving the power to execute it, and guaranteeing its success, is the King's assurance of his continued presence with his faithful followers.

———

Charles Spurgeon (CHS1, 258)

❖ ❖ ❖

All my friends are but One, but He is all sufficient.

———

William Carey (VLM, 15)

❖ ❖ ❖

This, we remember, is the great reward of the gospel: God himself. When we risk our lives to run after Christ, we discover the safety that is found only in his sovereignty, the security that is found only in his love, and the satisfaction that is found only in his presence. This is the eternally great reward, and we would be foolish to settle for anything less.

———

David Platt (181)

When he asks for and receives our all, He gives in
return that which is above price—his own presence.
The price is not great when compared with what
he gives in return; it is our blindness and our
unwillingness to yield that makes it seem great.

_____

Rosalind Goforth (EMQ4)

❖ ❖ ❖

Let but faithful labourers be found, who will prove
faithful to God, and there is no reason to fear that
God will not prove faithful to them.

_____

J. Hudson Taylor (AJB, 58)

PROVISION

It is true that we may desire much more. But let us use what we have, and God will give us more.

Adoniram Judson (CQ-AJ)

❖ ❖ ❖

Wants are things we think we need; necessities are things God knows we need. God will supply our needs, not our wants.

T. J. Bach (PMS, 41)

❖ ❖ ❖

God will not lead you where He will not provide for you.

David Sills (TMC)

"The Lord is my shepherd" is on Sunday, is on
Monday, and is through every day of the week; is in
January, is in December, and every month of the
year; is at home, and is in China; is in peace, and is
in war; in abundance, and in penury.

J. Hudson Taylor (DCQ-HT)

❖ ❖ ❖

We prefer one room in Rangoon to six in Boston.
We feel that we are highly blessed.

Adoniram Judson (LAJ, 146)

❖ ❖ ❖

The Gospel is free, but it takes money to keep the
Gospel Wagon in Tongaland.

Malla Moe (MOE, 209)

❖ ❖ ❖

All the resources of the Godhead are at our disposal!

Jonathan Goforth (RFM)

RECONCILIATION

Reconciliation in Christ will always result in reconciliation for Christ.

Patrick Fung (PF1)

❖   ❖   ❖

Reconciliation is the foundation of all Christian partnership. Reconciliation is to happen not only between ethnic groups, but also between generations, between the old and the young, and between genders. For the Spirit of God has been poured out on all peoples. God's new community includes those from the West and East, from the North and South, sons and daughters, young and old, men and women.

Patrick Fung (PF1)

This (God's) plan includes not only the reconciliation of people to God, but the reconciliation of "all things in heaven and on earth" (Eph 1:10). Or, as Paul puts it in Colossians 1:20, it is God's intention through Christ "to reconcile to himself all things, whether things on earth or things in heaven, by making peace through his blood, shed on the cross." Central to this plan is the reconciliation of persons to God through the blood of Jesus Christ. But the reconciliation won by Christ reaches to all the alienations that resulted from sin—alienation from ourselves, between people, and between humanity and the physical environment. As mind-boggling as the thought is, Scripture teaches that this reconciliation even includes the redemption of the physical universe from the effects of sin as everything is brought under its proper headship in Jesus Christ (Rom 8:19–21).

Howard A. Snyder (PWCM, 138)

Reconciliation is a position that Christ has achieved for us through the cross. We are reconciled to God. But we also know that in our human failures and weaknesses, reconciliation to one another sometimes is not evident; thus partnership becomes impossible. However, the foundation of all Christian partnership is reconciliation, and the foundation of reconciliation is the cross. The cross symbolizes death to self—death to our own rights just as Christ did.

Patrick Fung (PF1)

RELATIONSHIPS

Unless he (the leader) is constantly and faithfully wrestling in the heavenlies with the powers of darkness, there is real danger of his becoming involved in wrestling with his colleagues.

D. E. Hoste (DEH)

❖ ❖ ❖

Good missiology is made at the kitchen table. Meaningful missiology is made in the context of relationship. ... Relationship building is an essential part of our journey towards tomorrow.

Valdir Steuernagel (TGC, 180)

We do well to ask ourselves whether one reason for lack of greater progress and fruitfulness in our work may not be due to a lack of adjustment with some servants of the Lord. Are we prepared to take steps essential to healing such division?

D. E. Hoste (DEH)

❖ ❖ ❖

God has a significant role for you in his global mission. But it can be significant only if you are able to follow the servanthood of Jesus, which is difficult in the best of circumstances but especially challenging in places that are foreign to you. Yet God calls all Christians to this life and assures us that we will never be more like Jesus than when we serve.

Duane Elmer (CCS, 198)

❖ ❖ ❖

If we do not accept as good, God's shaping of our person and life in our own culture, we will never be able to accept his work in the lives of others who are culturally different from us.

Sherwood Lingenfelter and Marvin Mayers (CCS, 57)

RESOLVE

Nail the colors to the mast! That is the right thing to do, and, therefore, that is what we must do, and do it now. What colors? The colors of Christ, the work He has given us to do—the evangelization of all the unevangelized ... by faith in the omnipotence, fidelity, and wisdom of the Almighty Savior Who gave the command. Is there a wall in our path? By our God we will leap over it! Are there lions and scorpions in our way? We will trample them under our feet! Does a mountain bar our progress? Saying, "Be thou cast into the sea," we will march on. Soldiers of Jesus! Never surrender! Nail the colors to the mast!

C. T. Studd (CTS)

Lord, here in your precious Word I give myself, my
husband, my children, and all that I have or ever
shall possess, all to you. I will follow your will, even to
China. Lord, open doors, and I will go and tell the
Chinese of your great love. In time of need, supply
for us; in time of sorrow, give us peace; in times
of joy, send someone to share. Help me to never
murmur nor complain. I love you, Lord Jesus.
(This note comes from a page in Mrs. Collins' Bible
that was found at the scene of the airline crash in
Tibet in which the entire family perished in 1994.)

_____

Tanna Collins (DCQ)

❖ ❖ ❖

To obey was my objective,
To suffer was expected,
His glory was my reward,
His glory is my reward.

_____

Karen Watson, missionary martyr in Iraq (KW)

RESPONSIBILITY

If sinners be damned, at least let them leap to Hell over our bodies. If they will perish, let them perish with our arms about their knees. Let no one go there unwarned and unprayed for.

———

Charles Spurgeon (RF)

If you found a cure for cancer, wouldn't it be inconceivable to hide it from the rest of mankind? How much more inconceivable to keep silent the cure from the eternal wages of death.

———

Dave Davidson (SNU)

Going starts where we live, but it doesn't stop there. … If there are a billion people who have never heard the gospel and billions of others who still have not received the gospel, then we have an obligation to go to them. This is not an option. This is a command, not a calling. What is the matter of calling is where we will go and how long we will stay. We will not all go to the same places, and we will not all stay the same length of time. But it is clearly the will of God for us to take the gospel to the nations.

David Platt (RAD, 200)

❖ ❖ ❖

We talk of the Second Coming; half the world has never heard of the first.

Oswald J. Smith (GMN)

❖ ❖ ❖

What we can say for sure is that, at the very least, God calls every Christian to live with a missionary heart. God has called every Christian to international missions, but He does not want everyone to go. God calls some to be senders.

David Sills (TMC)

One who receives this Word, and by it salvation,
receives along with it the duty of passing this Word
on. ... Where there is no mission, there is no
Church, and where there is neither Church nor
mission, there is no faith.

Emil Brunner (WOQ)

❖   ❖   ❖

While vast continents are shrouded in darkness
... the burden of proof lies upon you to show that
the circumstances in which God has placed you
were meant by God to keep you out of the foreign
mission field.

Ion Keith-Falconer (WGD, 85)

❖   ❖   ❖

To stay here and disobey God—I can't afford to take
the consequence. I would rather go and obey God
than to stay here and know that I disobeyed.

Amanda Berry Smith (HM)

254

"Go ye" is as much a part of Christ's Gospel as
"Come unto Me." You are not even a Christian until
you have honestly faced your responsibility in regard
to the carrying of the Gospel to the ends of the earth.

J. Stuart Holden (HM)

❖   ❖   ❖

This generation of Christians is responsible for this
generation of souls on the earth!

Keith Green (SNU)

❖   ❖   ❖

I look on all the world as my parish; thus far I mean,
that, in whatever part of it I am, I judge it meet,
right, and my bounden duty, to declare unto all that
are willing to hear, the glad tidings of salvation.

John Wesley (JW)

❖   ❖   ❖

If God wills the evangelization of the world, and you
refuse to support missions, then you are opposed to
the will of God.

Oswald J. Smith (BCWE)

Our God of Grace often gives us a second chance,
but there is no second chance to harvest a ripe crop.

Kurt von Schleicher (GMN)

❖ ❖ ❖

We may not be able to prove from Scripture with
absolute certainty that no soul since Pentecost has
ever been saved by extraordinary means without the
knowledge of Christ. But neither can we prove from
Scripture that a single soul has been so saved ... for
me to propose it to other believers, to discuss it as a
possibility, is certainly dangerous, if not immoral.
It is almost as wrong as writing out such a hope so that
those who are under the judgment of God may read
it, take hope, and die. As long as the truth revealed to
us identifies only one way of escape, this is what
we must live by and proclaim.

Robertson McQuilkin (TGO, 50–51)

❖ ❖ ❖

We have all eternity to tell of victories won for
Christ, but we have only a few hours before sunset
to win them.

Jonathan Goforth (WR)

Any church that is not seriously involved in helping fulfill the Great Commission has forfeited its biblical right to exist.

Oswald J. Smith (SNU)

❖ ❖ ❖

Brother Andrew once asked while preaching in Sri Lanka, "What's the saddest verse in the Bible?" He answered his own question: "Psalm 142:4, 'no one cares for my soul.'" And he shared that when he first read the verse in his Bible, he wrote in the margin, "I don't want to be no one."

David Sunday (NCBC)

RISK TAKING

When you live by faith, it often feels like you are risking your reputation. You're not. You're risking God's reputation. It's not your faith that is on the line. It's His faithfulness. Why? Because God is the one who made the promise, and He is the only one who can keep it. The battle doesn't belong to you; it belongs to God. And because the battle doesn't belong to you, neither does the glory. God answers prayer to bring glory to His name, the name that is above all names.

Mark Batterson (TCM, Kindle location 3049)

❖ ❖ ❖

I am willing to fail. Risks are not to be evaluated in terms of the probability of their success, but in the value of the goal.

Ralph Winter (ITL, 189)

The greatest chapters in history always begin with
risk, and the same is true with the chapters of your
life. If you're unwilling to risk your reputation, you'll
never build the boat like Noah or get out of the boat
like Peter. You cannot build God's reputation if you
aren't willing to risk yours. There comes a moment
when you need to make the call or make the move.
Circle makers are risk takers.

Mark Batterson (TCM, Kindle location 569)

❖ ❖ ❖

If the fear of death paralyzes us, we will never venture
into the poor places, the violent places and the
dangerous places of the world—the places that are
most lacking in the knowledge of the good news of
Jesus Christ. Without risk-takers with eternity in
their hearts, who will reach the gangs of the cities, the
impoverished, those dying of AIDS, the terrorists?

Paul Borthwick (PB, 62)

❖ ❖ ❖

If we are going to wait until every possible hindrance
has been removed before we do a work for the Lord,
we will never attempt to do anything.

T. J. Bach (TET)

SACRIFICE

I will lay my bones by the Ganges that India might
know there is one who cares.

Alexander Duff (TET)

I never made a sacrifice. Of this we ought not to talk
when we remember the sacrifice which he made who
left his father's throne on high to give himself for us.

David Livingstone (EMQ3)

If Jesus Christ be God and died for me, then no
sacrifice can be too great for me to make for Him.

C. T. Studd (TTT)

Sacrifice also is an expression of your faith and confidence in God. You can give to others because you know that God will take care of you. And out of gratitude for God's great sacrifice in giving His Son so that you will be set free from the death sentence of sin, you give to others.

Crawford Loritts (LAI, 160)

❖ ❖ ❖

The less I spent on myself, the more I gave to others, the fuller of happiness and blessing did my soul become.

Hudson Taylor (HTSS, 27)

❖ ❖ ❖

Involvement in the global enterprise of following Christ always requires death in various shapes and sizes. Some will literally be asked to die (John 12:24), while others will be asked to die to selfishness, materialism, consumerism and all the other enemies of the Jesus-exalting gospel. Dietrich Bonhoeffer's most famous statement—"When Jesus calls a man, he bids him come and die"—urges us to take courage for the sake of Christ's kingdom.

Paul Borthwick (PB, 63)

Martyrdom has the power of revealing the love of
God to those in darkness. Herein lies its power to
convince and to persuade: people see the love of
God in the death of the martyr and are compelled to
believe in God's love and sacrifice for them.
Paul expressed the same idea in the concept of
reflecting the image of Christ or the glory of God to
other people through our suffering and our loving
self-sacrifice for others (2 Cor 3:18; 4:1–15). As the
knowledge of Christ and the grace of God is spread
to more and more people through the sacrifice
of the children of God, there is more and more
thanksgiving, praise, and glory given to God.

_____

Josef Tson (PWCM, 184)

❖ ❖ ❖

I don't think we are in any danger, and if we are,
we might as well die suddenly in God's work as by
some long drawn-out illness at home.

_____

Eleanor Chestnut, missionary martyr in China (AMG, 46)

❖ ❖ ❖

From my many years' experience I can unhesitatingly
say that the cross bears those who bear the cross.

_____

Sadhu Sundar Singh (SSS)

262

SACRIFICE

The challenge of the unoccupied fields of the world
is one to great faith and, therefore, to great sacrifice.
Our willingness to sacrifice for an enterprise is always
in proportion to our faith in that enterprise. Faith
has the genius of transforming the barely possible
into actuality. Once men are dominated by the
conviction that a thing must be done, they will
stop at nothing until it is accomplished.

Samuel M. Zwemer (SWZ1, 219)

❖　❖　❖

There are things you will have to give up when going
to a distant land for an extended period of time.
What you gain by leaving friends, family, home and
comforts is more than what you lose in staying with
them. God has given us a mission to take the Gospel
throughout the world. Our faithfulness to the Great
Commission has eternal rewards for us and eternal
consequences for those who hear the message.

Virgil Amos (AAE, 71)

There should be a law against the wholesale sacrifice
of life which is continually chronicled amongst
those who imagine they are "called" to labor in the
unhealthy climes as wives of missionaries.

From "The Boston Evening Transcript,"
regarding Emily Judson (MFL, 41)

❖ ❖ ❖

Our inadequate theology of heaven makes us run
from hardships. Not only do we fear death, but we
also avoid the necessary "dying to self" that comes
with following Jesus. We elude sacrifice, run from
pain and suffering, and live for the quickest results at
the minimum effort.

Paul Borthwick (PB, 57)

Self-Denial

True prosperity is being rightly related to God, being less self-serving, and fulfilling God's purpose in this generation.

Christopher J. H. Wright (CW)

❖ ❖ ❖

Life is pitiful, death so familiar, suffering and pain so common, yet I would not be anywhere else. Do not wish me out of this or in any way seek to get me out, for I will not be got out while this trial is on. These are my people, God has given them to me, and I will live or die with them for Him and His glory.

Gladys Aylward (EMT)

If missions languish, it is because the whole life of godliness is feeble. The command to go everywhere and preach to everybody is not obeyed until the will is lost by self-surrender in the will of God. Living, praying, giving and going will always be found together.

A. T. Pierson (SNU)

❖ ❖ ❖

When Paul was willing to suffer for Christ, he showed the nations that Christ is more precious than comfort and security and prosperity. In other words, the infinite value of the wisdom of God is revealed not in Paul's prosperity but in Paul's pain—in his prison. That's where it shines, because this is the wisdom of the cross, and we are called to pick up our crosses and display to the demons that we treasure Christ more than any human comfort.

John Piper (JP1)

❖ ❖ ❖

Is anything of value in Christ's service which costs little?

J. Hudson Taylor (SHT)

If these great things are to be achieved we must pay what it costs. What will be the price? Undoubtedly it involves giving ourselves to the study of missionary problems and strategy with all the thoroughness and tirelessness which have characterized the intellectual work of those men who have brought most benefit to mankind. It will cost genuine self-denial.

John R. Mott (SMZ2, 208)

SOCIAL CONCERN

One can't save and then pitchfork souls into heaven.
… Souls are more or less securely fastened to bodies.
… And as you can't get the souls out and deal with
them separately, you have to take them both together.

Amy Carmichael (TET)

❖ ❖ ❖

Poverty is rooted in broken relationships, so the
solution to poverty is rooted in the power of Jesus'
death and resurrection to put all things in right
relationship again.

Corbett and Fikkert (WHH, 38)

Today more than a billion people in the world live
and die in desperate poverty. They attempt to survive
on less than a dollar per day. If I am going to address
urgent spiritual need by sharing the gospel of Christ or
building up the body of Christ around the world, then
I cannot overlook dire physical need in the process.

David Platt (RAD, 108–109)

❖ ❖ ❖

An individual gospel without a social gospel is a
soul without a body, and a social gospel without an
individual gospel is a body without a soul. One is a
ghost and the other is a corpse.

E. Stanley Jones (QAM)

❖ ❖ ❖

I wonder if followers of Christ 150 years from now
will look back at Christians in America today and ask,
"How could they live in such big houses? How could
they drive such nice cars and wear such nice clothes?
How could they live in such affluence while thousands
of children were dying because they didn't have food
and water? How could they go on with their lives as
though the billions of poor didn't even exist?"

David Platt (RAD, 111)

The nature of love is to do good and to relieve need.
If, then, our neighbor is unconverted, we are to
show love ... by seeking to share with him the good
news without which he will perish. So, we find Paul
warning and teaching "everyone" (Col 1:28). Not
merely because he was an apostle. but because every
man was his neighbor.

J. I. Packer (JIP1, 108–109)

❖ ❖ ❖

What, then, is the biblical basis for social concern?
Why should Christians get involved? In the end there
are only two possible attitudes which Christians can
adopt towards the world: Escape and Engagement. ...
"Escape" means turning our backs on the world in
rejection, washing our hands of it ... and steeling our
hearts against its agonized cries for help. In contrast,
"engagement" means turning our faces towards the
world in compassion, getting our hands dirty, sore
and worn in its service, and feeling deep within us the
stirring of the love of which cannot be contained.

John R. W. Stott (DCQ)

Some of us are world-centered; our challenge is to balance that with empathy and care for the needy and broken. For those in ministries of compassion, our challenge may be to ensure we sensitively, compassionately and wisely but also verbally communicate the gospel. Our model is Jesus who both spoke to and fed the five thousand.

Lindsay Brown (LB)

❖   ❖   ❖

Although we cannot be saved by good works, we also cannot be saved without them. Good works are not the way of salvation, but its proper and necessary evidence. A faith which does not express itself in works is dead.

John R. W. Stott (MGP, 195)

Spiritual Warfare

The trumpet still plays the notes of war. You cannot sit down and put the victory wreath on your head. You do not have a crown. You still must wear the helmet and carry the sword. You must watch, pray, and fight. Expect your last battle to be the most difficult, for the enemy's fiercest charge is reserved for the end of the day.

Charles Spurgeon (CHS)

❧ ❧ ❧

I have ever found that when I have thought the battle was over and the conquest gained, and so let down my watch, the enemy has risen up and done me the greatest injury.

David Brainerd (JDB, 118)

We must recognize that the Church's real battle is not with fellow Christians "but against principalities, against powers, against the rulers of the darkness of this age" (Eph 6:12). How we as a Church fight this cosmic battle is a cosmic matter, and the armor of God is our spiritual equipment that moves us forward to victory.

Ramez Atallah (RA1)

❖ ❖ ❖

Spiritual warfare is not about naming territorial spirits, claiming the ground or binding demons. It is all about the gospel. It is to live a gospel life, to preserve gospel unity and to proclaim gospel truth. It is to do this in the face of a hostile world, a deceptive enemy and our own sinful natures. And it is to pray to a sovereign God for gospel opportunities. Advance comes through godliness, unity, proclamation and prayer.

Timothy Chester (MGP, 260)

How shall we view the world of missions? In the
first place, it is not an organizational or religious
effort. World missions is not, strictly speaking, the
work of the Church, but the work of God. World
missions means the invasion of God into a hostile
world—a world filled with fiendish forces, filled with
demonized forces of hell in black array.

———

L. E. Maxwell (FUT, 161)

❖ ❖ ❖

How then must we view world missions? Is it a job?
A business? A service? A mission? A commission?
An assignment? A program? An investment?
Perhaps in a measure, these things, but missions
must be first a campaign, a conquest, a war. If it
is not first that, it will never be realized in these
other respects. World missions means war, total
war and mobilization. The Governor General of
this campaign is none other than the Captain of
our salvation.

———

L. E. Maxwell (FUT, 161)

Some say this is the greatest investment in which you can put your time, substance, and life. Nonsense! It's a war! I don't like to hear missions described as a business investment, for there are two implications that I believe are wrong. First, when someone asks me to make an investment, I expect in reasonable time some returns. In the second place, the implication is that what I have I can choose to do with as I will. And that's not so either. Total warfare means total commitment with no options and no returns, and past the point of no return.

Francis Steele (FUT, 161–162)

STRATEGY

Without pastoral training and theological education for oral learners, it would be hard for a leader to care for a church. The challenge is for the missionary-trainer to contextualize teaching, but to assume and encourage a literacy improvement among the national leaders. One of the greatest social ministries we can offer on the mission field today is literacy training and not assume that leaders will want to continue to be oral learners. The Bible was written down, and I think we must remember that the Lord, in His wisdom, had it written, thus showing a benefit in moving the redeemed and their ecclesiastical leaders toward literacy.

David Bledsoe (R&T, 181)

The Gospel must be constantly forwarded to a new
address because its recipient is repeatedly changing
his place of residence.

Helmut Thielicke (P&C, 160)

❖ ❖ ❖

I am concerned that we as Asians may be repeating
the same mistake that our Western brethren might
have committed in the past; that is, to equate
economic and political power with advances in the
spreading of the gospel. We continue to reinforce
the notion that the spreading of the gospel is always
from the powerful to the powerless, the haves to the
have-nots. There is a sense of Asian triumphalism
that makes me nervous.

Patrick Fung (PF1)

❖ ❖ ❖

One thing is clear, receptivity wanes as often as
it waxes. Like the tide, it comes in and goes out.
Unlike the tide, no one can guarantee when it goes
out that it will soon come back again.

Donald A. McGavran (UCG, 181)

I simply argue that the cross should be raised at the center of the marketplace as well as on the steeple of the church. I am recovering the claim that Jesus was not crucified in a cathedral between two candles, but on a cross between two thieves; on the town's garbage heap; at a crossroad so cosmopolitan they had to write His title in Greek ... at the kind of a place where cynics talk smut and thieves curse and soldiers gamble. Because that is where He died. And that is what He died for. And that is what He died about. This is where churchmen ought to be and what churchmen ought to be about.

George MacLeod (CFU, 98)

❖   ❖   ❖

Right strategy tailors mission to fit each of the thousands of separate communities, so that in it the church may grow.

Donald McGavran (EMQ3)

SUFFERING
(PERSECUTION)

Endeavor to rejoice in every loss and suffering
incurred for Christ's sake and the gospel's,
remembering that though, like death, they are not
to be willfully incurred, yet, like death, they are
great gain.

Adoniram Judson (LAJ, 315)

❖ ❖ ❖

Suffering and success go together. If you are
succeeding without suffering, it is because others
before you have suffered; if you are suffering without
succeeding, it is that others after you may succeed.

Edward Judson, Adoniram's son (EJ)

God's plan is that his saving purpose for the nations
will triumph through the suffering of his people,
especially his frontline forces who break through the
darkness of Satan's blinding hold on an unreached
people. That is what the lives of William Tyndale,
John Paton, and Adoniram Judson illustrate so
dramatically.

John Piper (FUAC, 26)

❖ ❖ ❖

We will never know from experience God's richest
blessings of comfort and compassion toward others
until we ourselves have had trials.

T. J. Bach (CT)

❖ ❖ ❖

God appoints suffering and prayer as means of
gathering the nations into the unsearchable riches
of the glory of God's wisdom. Suffering and prayer,
prison and prayer, are appointed by God. When
Paul was willing to go to prison for the sake of
Christ, he showed the nations that Christ is more
precious than freedom.

John Piper (JP1)

We must be careful when we say, "God has a wonderful plan for your life." God does have a wonderful plan, and you can be part of that plan, but it may not be wonderful for you.

Charles Price (CP)

❖ ❖ ❖

We must never minimize the suffering of another. Scripture's mandate to us is, "Weep with them that weep" (Rom 12:15, KJV).

Billy Graham (DCQ)

❖ ❖ ❖

The place of suffering in service and of passion in mission is hardly ever taught today. But the greatest single secret of evangelistic or missionary effectiveness is the willingness to suffer and die. It may be a death to popularity (by the use of modest methods in reliance on the Holy Spirit), or to racial and national prejudice (by identification with another culture), or to material comfort (by adopting a simpler lifestyle). But the servant must suffer if he is to bring light to the nations, and the seed must die if it is to multiply.

John R. W. Stott (MGP, 240)

Are we partakers of Christ's sufferings? Are we prepared for God to stamp out our personal ambitions? Are we prepared for God to destroy our individual decisions by supernaturally transforming them? It will mean not knowing why God is taking us that way, because knowing would make us spiritually proud. We never realize at the time what God is putting us through—we go through it more or less without understanding. Then suddenly we come to a place of enlightenment, and realize—"God has strengthened me and I didn't even know it!"

Oswald Chambers (MUFH1)

❖   ❖   ❖

The glue that united Paul's thought and life with the message he preached and the mission he conducted was his suffering as an apostle of Jesus Christ. Paul's suffering was the vehicle through which the saving power of God, climactically revealed in Christ, was being made known in the world. To reject the suffering Paul was therefore to reject Christ; to identify with Paul in his suffering was a sure sign that one was being saved by the "foolishness" and "stumbling-block" of the cross.

Scott Hafemann (MGP, 240)

Finally we note that God, in order to enable a new creation which transcends the present order of suffering and death, engages in such a giving of self that only one of the sharpest of human pains known can adequately portray what is involved for God. But such an event is not thought of solely in terms of the internal life of God. God's suffering is the heavenly counterpart to the suffering of the earthly servant of God. The suffering servant takes upon himself the suffering of God and does what is finally necessary for the forces of evil in this world to be overcome: suffering unto death.

Terence Fretheim (MGP, 241)

❖ ❖ ❖

The Church has been and always will be persecuted. Everyone watches us. If we die in faith, hope, and love, it can change the history of nations. If we fail to stand in love and hope and for our faith, nations often can reject Christ.

Anonymous missionary
who works in China and North Korea

If I had not felt certain that every additional trial was ordered by infinite love and mercy, I could not have survived my accumulated suffering.

Adoniram Judson (TTJ, 40)

❖ ❖ ❖

In spite of sorrow, loss, and pain,
Our course be onward still;
We sow on Burma's barren plain,
We reap on Zion's hill.

Adoniram Judson (RR)

❖ ❖ ❖

If we live for God we must suffer persecution. The kingdom of darkness and the kingdom of light are at war. ... As long as the kingdom of darkness is permitted to exist, there will be a conflict, and ... if you want to be popular in heaven, and get a reward that shall last forever, you will have to be unpopular here.

D. L. Moody (DLM, 93)

The dangers that exist are real, but only illustrate the fact that men and women need Christ. The suffering and dying of missionaries advance the Kingdom as nothing else could and the blood of the saints has ever been the seed and fuel of gospel advance.

David Sills (TMC)

❖ ❖ ❖

Grace is costly because it calls us to follow, and it is grace because it calls us to follow Jesus Christ. It is costly because it costs a man his life, and it is grace because it gives a man the only true life. It is costly because it condemns sin, and grace because it justifies the sinner. Above all, it is costly because it cost God the life of His son: "Ye were bought at a price" and what has cost God much cannot be cheap for us. Above all, it is grace because God did not reckon his Son too dear a price to pay for our life, but delivered Him up for us. Costly grace is the incarnation of God.

Dietrich Bonhoeffer (COD)

Suffering for Christ is not only the suffering of persecution. It begins when one leaves close relatives for the service of Christ. For some, it means selling their possessions and giving them to the poor, which often means giving them for the propagation of the gospel. For others, suffering for Christ may mean agonizing in prayer for the cause of Christ, or agonizing and toiling for the building up of the body of Christ and the perfecting of the saints. Again, to clarify this concept, suffering for Christ is not a self-inflicted suffering. The disciple of Christ seeks to do the will of Christ and to promote the cause of Christ. However, suffering for Christ does mean that the disciple will voluntarily involve himself in suffering and in sacrificial living for Christ and His gospel.

Josef Tson (PWCM, 181)

Jesus Christ as the King of kings and Lord of lords, calls people to Himself and demands from them total allegiance to Himself. ... He expects them to meet that hatred with love, and to face that violence with glad acceptance, following His example by suffering and dying for the lost world. Their suffering and martyrdom are prompted by their allegiance to His own Person and are endured for the purpose of spreading His gospel. Christ's disciples do not seek these things for their own sake, and they do not inflict these on themselves. Their goal is not to suffer and to die; on the contrary, their goal is Christ's Person and Christ's cause in the world, the spreading of His gospel.

Josef Tson (PWCM, 181)

❖ ❖ ❖

Christ's presence has turned my prison into a blessed heaven. What then will His presence do for me in heaven hereafter?

Sadhu Sundar Singh, from prison (BSWE)

With him, my beloved Master, it is good everywhere. With him I have light in the dark dungeon. I had asked him to be where I am needed, not where it is better for the outward man, but where I can bear fruit. This is my calling.

Russian Pastor P. Rumatchik, from a letter written when imprisoned for the fifth time (TO, 233)

❖ ❖ ❖

I can think of nothing that would make death more welcomed than to meet it here, to die for these dear children as my Savior died for me. It is the suffering and dying Savior that melts the stony heart. So with us—that which our lives cannot do our deaths may do.

Ella Schenck, missionary martyr in Sierra Leone (AMG, 101)

God has chosen that some of his servants be imprisoned as a way of bringing about his cosmic purpose.

———

John Piper (JP1)

❖ ❖ ❖

More and more I am persuaded from Scripture and from the history of missions that God's design for the evangelization of the world and the consummation of his purposes includes the suffering of his ministers and missionaries. To put it more plainly and specifically, God designs that the suffering of his ambassadors is one essential means in the triumphant spread of the Good News among all the peoples of the world.

———

John Piper (FUAC, 14)

However, when the ambassador of Christ speaks the truth in love, and meets death with joy, a strange miracle occurs: the eyes of unbelievers are opened, they are enabled to see the truth of God, and this leads them to believe in the gospel. Ever since the centurion's eyes were opened at Calvary, ever since he believed that Jesus was the Son of God *because* he had seen *the manner of His death* (Mark 15:39), thousands and thousands of Christian martyrdoms over the centuries have produced the same results. Moreover, this was precisely what Tertullian had in mind when he wrote that the blood of the martyrs is the seed out of which new Christians are born. Many, many groups of people on this planet have testified that the darkness which had been over them was dissipated only when a missionary was killed there. However, countless areas and peoples of the world today so experience a darkness that will be vanquished only when enough Christians have given up their lives in martyrdom.

Josef Tson (PWCM, 183)

SURRENDER

I had utterly abandoned myself to Him. … Could any choice be as wonderful as His will? Could any place be safer than the center of His will? Did not He assure me by His very Presence that His thoughts towards us are good, and not evil? Death to my own plans and desires was almost deliriously delightful. Everything was laid at His nail-scarred feet, life or death, health or illness, appreciation by others or misunderstanding, success or failure as measured by human standards. Only He Himself mattered.

V. Raymond Edman (BSWE)

❖　❖　❖

Live to be forgotten, so Christ can be remembered.

D. E. Hoste (PF2)

The meaning of being a Christian is that in
response for the gift of a whole Christ,
I give my whole self to Him.

Alexander MacLaren (AMac)

❖ ❖ ❖

The biggest hindrance to the missionary task is self.
Self that refuses to die. Self that refuses to sacrifice.
Self that refuses to give. Self that refuses to go.

Thomas Hale (OBM, 29)

❖ ❖ ❖

Give me the love that leads the way,
The faith that nothing can dismay,
The hope no disappointments tire,
The passion that will burn like fire;
Let me not sink to be a clod:
Make me Thy fuel, Flame of God!

Amy Carmichael (AC)

❖ ❖ ❖

All failure in caring, giving, praying and living for
missions is owing to a weak, superficial spiritual life.

Andrew Murray (AM, 63)

The presence of God became unutterably real and
blessed, and I remember … stretching myself on the
ground and lying there before Him with unspeakable
awe and unspeakable joy. For what service I was
accepted I knew not, but a deep consciousness that
I was not my own took possession of me which has
never since been effaced.

J. Hudson Taylor (HTSS, 19–20)

❖ ❖ ❖

Hudson Taylor's experience shows us how God
trains a man to believe in Him, to wait on Him,
to give himself up entirely to His will and service,
however great the difficulty may be. The Church
needs to learn the lesson, our missionary meetings
and our mission sermons must aim at teaching that,
as individuals give themselves wholly to God, He
will equip them for being used in the service of His
kingdom. … And it requires close communion with
God, and a full surrender to His guidance, to fit us
to do His work.

Andrew Murray (AM, 77)

The only way to waken true, deep, spiritual, permanent missionary interest is not to aim at this itself so much as to lead believers to a more complete separation from the world, and to an entire consecration of themselves, with all they have, to their Lord and His service.

Andrew Murray (AM, 55)

❖ ❖ ❖

I have nothing to do with how long I shall live. I am in the will of God. If He sees fit to let me live to complete the language and to present the Lord Jesus and His power to save, I shall be happy. If not, His will be done. Do you not know that a grave often speaks louder than life?

Arthur Tylee, missionary martyr in the Amazon
(AMG, 169)

❖ ❖ ❖

I have been crucified with Christ. It is no longer I who live, but Christ who lives in me. And the life I now live in the flesh I live by faith in the Son of God, who loved me and gave himself for me.

Apostle Paul (Gal 2:20)

294

We do not lose heart. Though our outer self is
wasting away, our inner self is being renewed
day by day. For this light momentary affliction is
preparing for us an eternal weight of glory beyond all
comparison, as we look not to the things that are seen
but to the things that are unseen. For the things that
are seen are transient, but the things that are unseen
are eternal.

Apostle Paul (2 Cor 4:16–18)

❖ ❖ ❖

Lord, I give up
All my own plans and purposes,
All my own desires and hopes
And accept Thy will for my life.
I give myself, my life, my all,
Utterly to Thee
To be Thine forever.
Fill me and seal me with Thy Holy Spirit.
Use me as Thou wilt,
Send me where Thou wilt,
Work out Thy whole will in my life
At any cost,
Now and forever.
To me to live is Christ. Amen.

Betty Scott Stam, missionary martyr in China (AMG, 75)

295

God first wants our availability, then our mobility, and finally our ability.

Charles Price, Pastor, People's Church, Toronto, Canada (CP)

❖ ❖ ❖

The situation in Nicaragua is getting worse. If Nicaragua falls, I guess the rest of Central America will, too. Maybe this is just some kind of self-inflicted martyr complex, but I find this recurring thought that perhaps God will call me to be martyred for Him in His service in Colombia. I am willing.

Chet Bitterman, missionary martyr in Colombia (CTD)

❖ ❖ ❖

I place no value on anything I have or may possess, except in relation to the kingdom of Christ. If anything will advance the interests of the kingdom, it shall be given away or kept, only as by giving or keeping it I shall most promote the glory of him to whom I owe all my hopes in time and eternity.

David Livingstone (TC)

To summarize, we affirm an incarnational model of mission understood as humble self-renunciation for the sake of others whereby the life and love of Christ become manifest to others. Mission in the spirit of Christ is an undertaking of selfless love, a surrender of rights and privileges, in order to serve and identify with others for the sake of the gospel. Incarnational mission profoundly defines the character of mission, which in turn impacts our understanding, our method, and our commitment in mission.

Craig Ott (ETM, 104)

❖ ❖ ❖

Let there be no reservation; give yourselves up fully and wholly to Him whose you are and whom you wish to serve in this work; and then there can be no disappointment.

J. Hudson Taylor (AJB, 358)

❖ ❖ ❖

Like the cold of snow in the time of harvest is a faithful messenger to those who send him;
he refreshes the soul of his masters.

King Solomon (Prov 25:13)

It is sweet to be nothing and less than nothing that Christ may be all in all.

David Brainerd (IMG, 22)

❖ ❖ ❖

God takes great pleasure in manifesting His presence and pouring out His power on those who will dare to align radically their purposes with His for the nations.

Steve Childers (RTS)

❖ ❖ ❖

The message I would leave with you as I set forth a second time to bear His message again is the same as someone has said: "In like manner as David Livingstone went out of Africa praying, so ought a man to enter." So on bended knee and with heart bowed to God in submission to His will, I bid you farewell.

Hulda Stumpf, missionary martyr in Kenya (AMG, 106)

We are living in interesting times over here, and I
believe the missionaries are going to see real persecution
before the thing is over. ... But it is one of the greatest
privileges I can think of to be here as a missionary. ...
We hope to see you all again, but, if we should be denied
that blessed joy, we can meet again in that land which
is fairer than day. May we strive harder to be worthy of
the world which God has given us and of that other land
made possible through our Lord Jesus Christ.

Erle Rounds, missionary martyr in the Philippines (AMG, 142)

❖　❖　❖

When God chose to bring salvation to you and me,
he did not send gold or silver, cash or check. He
sent himself—the Son. If we are going to accomplish
the global purpose of God, it will not be primarily
through giving our money, as important as that is. It
will happen primarily through giving ourselves.

David Platt (RAD, 198)

Nobody chooses to go to prison. Nobody chooses
to walk away from prosperity. Nobody can see the
breadth and length and height and depth of the
love of Christ so fully that they're willing. Nobody
says with the apostle Paul, "I count everything as
loss for the surpassing greatness of knowing Christ
our Lord." Nobody talks like that unless divine,
supernatural, sovereign power has broken into their
lives, and God has ordained that it come into their
lives through prayer.

John Piper (JP1)

❖ ❖ ❖

Who is there who can always see the shadow of the
cross falling upon his bank account? Who is there
who has the mark of the nails and the print of the
spear in his plans and life, his love and devotion and
daily program of intercession? Who is there who has
heard the word of Jesus and is quietly, obediently,
every day, as He has told you and me, taking up his
cross to follow Him?

Samuel M. Zwemer (BOY, 199)

I was a free man in a good position, and I bargained away my noble status—and I am not ashamed of this or regretful about it—for the sake of others. In short, I am a slave of Christ in a remote country because of the unspeakable glory of eternal life which is in Christ Jesus our Lord.

Patrick of Ireland (TGC, 94)

❖   ❖   ❖

Just one life. This is all any one of us has to offer. How can it be used for the greatest glory of God and the greatest blessing to men? How can we be as useful as possible and as effective as possible as Christians?

Michael Griffiths (MG, 10)

❖   ❖   ❖

When James Calvert went out as a missionary to the cannibals of the Fiji Islands, the ship captain tried to turn him back, saying, "You will lose your life and the lives of those with you if you go among such savages." To that, Calvert replied, "We died before we came here."

Unknown (BSWE)

With the world under his feet, with heaven in his eye, with the gospel in his hand and Christ in his head, he pleads as an ambassador for God, knowing nothing but Jesus Christ, enjoying nothing but the conversion of sinners, hoping for nothing but the promotion of the kingdom of Christ, and glorying in nothing but in the cross of Christ Jesus, by which he is crucified to the world, and the world to him.

Henry Venn, 1805 (ETM,189)

❦ ❦ ❦

Dick (former TEAM General Director) and Marjorie Winchell released their rights in another way. As a middle-aged couple, they actively released their children to the service of Christ abroad. They knew that this would mean times of loneliness and longing for their family members, but when their children were still young Marjorie and Dick had prayed, "Lord, we ask that we won't get to meet our grandchildren until our children are home on their first furlough from overseas cross-cultural service."

Paul Borthwick (PB)

THEOLOGY
(THEOLOGY OF MISSIONS)

The cross is the unavoidable center of our mission.
All Christian mission flows from the cross—as its
source, its power, and as that which defines its scope.
It is vital that we see the cross as central and integral
to every aspect of holistic biblical mission, that is, of
all we do in the name of the crucified and risen Jesus.

Christopher J. H. Wright (MOG, 314)

❖   ❖   ❖

Missiology apart from a sound theology is a
dangerous and speculative undertaking. Not only
does theology help us to correctly interpret the
scriptures, but it also provides the larger framework
of biblical understanding with which a theology of
mission must be in harmony.

Craig Ott (ETM, xix)

Biblical theology of mission provides the *North Star* by which the ship of mission must navigate. Though storms may rage and currents may pull, the ship of mission can stay its intended course as long as it reorients itself on the fixed point. Trends and fads, political correctness, popular opinion (inside and outside the church), ethnocentrism and myopia, and a host of other forces would blow this ship off course. The scriptures as the revealed Word of God must remain the fixed point by which we navigate the ship of mission.

Craig Ott (ETM, xxi–xxii)

Sin made salvation necessary and sin makes Christian missions necessary. ... Sin is written in bold letters upon the pages of the Bible. Only four chapters are exempt from this evil. According to Genesis 1–2, sin was not a part of original human history. Neither is it found in Revelation 21–22. There is thus a brief pre-sin history (Gen 1–2) and post-sin history (Rev 21–22). The rest of the Bible (Gen 3–Rev 20) is a record of human sin and divine intervention, preparation, accomplishment and actualization of salvation.

George Peters (BTM, 15)

VISION

In the vast plain to the north I have sometimes seen,
in the morning sun, the smoke of a thousand villages
where no missionary has ever been.

Robert Moffat (BSWE)

❖ ❖ ❖

If every Christian is already considered a missionary,
then all can stay put where they are, and nobody
needs to get up and go anywhere to preach the gospel.
But if our only concern is to witness where we are,
how will people in unevangelized areas ever hear
the gospel? The present uneven distribution of
Christians and opportunities to hear the gospel of
Christ will continue on unchanged.

Gordon Olson (WGD, 12)

We have a whole Christ for our salvation; a whole
Bible for our staff; a whole church for our fellowship;
and a whole world for our parish.

John Chrysostom (EMQ3)

❖ ❖ ❖

I like men whose vision carries them far beyond their
own horizons.

Kenneth Strachan (TET)

❖ ❖ ❖

A vision without a task makes a visionary.
A task without a vision makes drudgery.
A vision with a task makes a missionary!

Samuel Chadwick (SL, chapter 8)

WORSHIP & MISSIONS

Worship involves witness. The factor which unites them is the name of God. For what is worship but to "glory in His holy name," to "praise," "bless," or "stand in awe of" it? And what is witness but to "proclaim the name of the Lord" to others? These expressions are found in the Psalter, and it is in the Psalms that the proper combination of worship and witness is most clearly and commonly found. ... Worship is "worth-ship," and acknowledgement of the worth of Almighty God. ... It is therefore impossible for me to worship God and yet not care two cents whether anybody else worships Him too. ... Worship which does not beget witness is hypocrisy. We cannot acclaim the worth of God if we have no desire to proclaim it.

Christopher J. H. Wright (MGP, 251)

May his name endure forever,
his fame continue as long as the sun!
May people be blessed in him,
all nations call him blessed!
Blessed be the Lord, the God of Israel,
who alone does wondrous things.
Blessed be his glorious name forever;
may the whole earth be filled with his glory!
Amen and Amen!

King David's Psalm for Solomon (Ps 72:17–19)

❖   ❖   ❖

The opposite of disrespect (for God) is worship.
Worship is not a gathering. It is not essentially a
song service or sitting under preaching. Worship is
not essentially any form of outward act. Worship is
essentially an inner stirring of the heart to treasure
God above all the treasures of the world—
  a valuing of God above all else that is valuable
  a loving of God above all else that is lovely
  a savoring of God above all else that is sweet
  an admiring of God above all else that is admirable
  a fear of God above all else that is fearful
  a respecting of God above all else that is respectable
  a prizing of God above all else that is precious.

John Piper (LNBG, 206)

God is pursuing with omnipotent passion a worldwide purpose of gathering joyful worshipers for Himself from every tribe and tongue and people and nation. He has an inexhaustible enthusiasm for the supremacy of His name among the nations. Therefore, let us bring our affections into line with His, and, for the sake of His name, let us renounce the quest for worldly comforts and join His global purpose.

John Piper (LNBG, 43)

❧ ❧ ❧

If the pursuit of God's glory is not ordered above the pursuit of man's good in the affections of the heart and the priorities of the church, man will not be well served and God will not be duly honored. I am not pleading for a diminishing of missions but for a magnifying of God. When the flame of worship burns with the heat of God's true worth, the light of missions will shine to the darkest peoples on earth. And I long for that day to come!

John Piper (LNBG, 18)

Missions is not the ultimate goal of the Church.
Worship is. Missions exists because worship doesn't.
Worship is ultimate, not missions, because God is
ultimate, not man. When this age is over, and the
countless millions of the redeemed fall on their
faces before the throne of God, missions will be no
more. It is a temporary necessity. But worship abides
forever. ... Worship, therefore, is the fuel and goal of
missions. It's the goal of missions because in missions
we simply aim to bring the nations into the white-hot
enjoyment of God's glory. The goal of missions is the
gladness of the people in the greatness of God.

_____

John Piper (LNBG, 17)

❖ ❖ ❖

My heaven is to please God and glorify him, and to
give all to him, and to be wholly devoted to his glory;
that is the heaven I long for.

_____

David Brainerd (TGC, 108)

The very nature of God, God's majesty and goodness,
evoke adoration and gratitude. Such a response serves
to honour God while proclaiming to all who hear that
this YHWH God is worthy of one's love and fidelity.
Hence praise is not only devotion but also testimony,
both an exalting of God and a proclamation that
seeks to draw others into the worship of God.

Samuel E. Balentine (MGP, 247)

❖ ❖ ❖

May God be gracious to us and bless us
and make his face to shine upon us,
that your way may be known on earth,
your saving power among all nations.
Let the peoples praise you, O God;
let all the peoples praise you!
Let the nations be glad and sing for joy,
for you judge the peoples with equity
and guide the nations upon earth.
Let the peoples praise you, O God;
let all the peoples praise you!
The earth has yielded its increase;
God, our God, shall bless us.
God shall bless us;
let all the ends of the earth fear him!

Psalm 67

APPENDIX

"*Expect Great Things; Attempt Great Things*"
—WILLIAM CAREY, 1792

"*Expect great things; attempt great things,*" the quotation attributed to William Carey, has a mixed literary history. Originally spoken in his sermon to the Baptist Association meeting in Northampton, England, May 30, 1792, Carey used the citation to urge his Baptist colleagues to enter the missionary enterprise. William Finnemore (*The Story of a Hundred Years: 1823–1923*, Oxford: University Press, 1923, 14) suggested that the saying formed the twofold division of Carey's sermon.

The significance and contemporary use of Carey's proverbial saying continues. For example, on February 20, 2001, The Reverend Doctor George L. Carey (no relation to William Carey), former archbishop of Canterbury, Church of England, urged Nigerian Anglicans to trust in God and to expect great things from God. In addition, numerous educational institutions and churches use Carey's saying as a motto.

Various forms of the saying appear in the sources, but the most probable form was "*Expect great things; attempt great things.*" Among others, William Staughton, one of the founding members of the Baptist Missionary Society in 1792, cites Carey's saying in the short form.

Following are listed the various forms of the saying and the sources:

Expect great things—attempt great things.

- Narrative of the First Establishment of this Society." Periodical Accounts Relative to A Society, Formed Among The Particular Baptists, for Propagating the Gospel Among the Heathen, No. I. In *Periodical Accounts Relative to the Baptist Missionary Society*, Vol. I (Clipston: Printed by J. W. Morris, 1800), 3.

- William Staughton, *The Baptist Mission in India: Containing a Narrative of Its Rise, Progress, and Present Condition, A Statement of the Physical and Moral Character of the Hindoos, Their Cruelties, Tortures and Burnings, With a Very Interesting Description of Bengal* (Philadelphia: Hellings and Aitken, 1811), Title page, 1.

- Miron Winslow, *A Sketch of Missions; or History of the Principal Attempts to Propagate Christianity among the Heathen* (Andover, Massachusetts: Flagg and Gould, 1819), 250–251.

313

- John Scott, *The Life of the Rev. Thomas Scott, D.D., Rector of Aston Sandford, Bucks; Including a Narrative Drawn Up By Himself, and Copious Extracts of His Letters* (Boston: Samuel T. Armstrong and Crocker & Brewster; New York: John P. Haven, 1822), 125 [this account states that Andrew Fuller reported this form of the saying to Rev. Thomas Scott].

- Eustace Carey and William Yates, *Vindication of the Calcutta Baptist Missionaries: In Answer to "A Statement relative to Serampore, by J. Marshman, D.D. with Introductory Observations by John Foster"* (London: Wightman & Co. and Parbury, 1828), Title page, 34– 35.

- *The Baptist Magazine for 1830*, Vol. XXII (London: George Wightman, July 1830), 311.

- "Biographical Sketch of The Rev. William Carey, D.D., Late Principal of Serampore College, Bengal," *The Congregational Magazine, for the Year 1835* (January 1835), 3.

- John Dyer, "The Rev. Doctor Carey, Professor of Oriental Languages in the College of Fort William, Calcutta, &c, &c." In *The Christian Keepsake, and Missionary Annual,* ed. by William Ellis (London, Paris, and America: Fisher, Son, & Co., 1837), Title page, 11.

APPENDIX

- "Dr. Marshman" [Obituary]. *The Museum of Foreign Literature, Science and Art*, Vol. V, New Series, Vol. XXXIII, ed. by Robert Walsh, Eliakim Littell, and John Jay Smitt (Philadelphia: E. Littell, & Co., 1838), 419; reprint, *The Friend of India*, December, 1837.

- *The American Quarterly Register*. Conducted by B. B. Edwards and W. Cogswell, published by the American Education Society, Vol. XI (Boston: Perkins & Marvin, 1839), 57.

- "The Jubilee." In *The Missionary Herald*, No. 36, May 1842. Reprinted in *The Baptist Magazine for 1842*, Vol. XXXIV (London: Houlston and Stoneman), 267.

- Rev. Benjamin Godwin, "The Goodness of God Reviewed, and the Hand of God Acknowledged." In *Two Sermons Preached at Kettering on the 31st of May, and the 1st of June, 1842, before the Baptist Missionary Society, Special General Meeting Held in Celebration of the Fiftieth Year; With an Account of the Meeting* (London: The Society's House and Houlston and Stoneman, 1842), 3.

- Rev. Edward Steane, "The Present Position of the Missionary Enterprise, Contrasted with Its Commencement." In *Two Sermons Preached at Kettering on the 31st of May, and the 1st of June, 1842, before the Baptist Missionary Society, Special General Meeting Held in Celebration of the Fiftieth Year; With an Account of the Meeting* (London: The Society's House and Houlston and Stoneman, 1842), 58.

- Holmes and Co., *The Bengal Obituary, or a Record to Perpetuate the Memory of Departed Worth, Being a Compilation of Tablets and Monumental Inscriptions from Various parts of the Bengal and Agra Presidencies. To which is Added Biographical Sketches and Memoirs of Such as Have Pre-Eminently Distinguished Themselves in the History of British India, since the Formation of the European Settlement to the Present Time* (Calcutta: J. Thomas, Baptist Mission Press, 1848), 335, 341.

- *The Primitive Methodist Magazine for the Year of Our Lord 1855*, Vol. XIII of the Third Series, Vol. XXXVI from the Commencement (London: Thomas King, [1855]), 666.

- John Clark Marshman, *The Life and Times of Carey, Marshman, and Ward Embracing the History of the Serampore Mission*, Vol. II (London: Longman, Brown, Green, Longmans, and Roberts, 1859), 506.

- M. J. Knowlton, "The Ningpo Mission and Our Duty," *The Missionary Magazine* XVIII/9 (September 1863), 336.

- Leighton and Mornay Williams, eds., *Serampore Letters, Being the unpublished correspondence of William Carey and others with John Williams, 1800–1816*, with an introduction by Thomas Wright (New York and London: G. P. Putnam's Sons, 1892), 9.

Attempt great things; expect great things.

- *The Latter Day Luminary, by a Committee of the Baptist Board of Foreign Missions* (Philadelphia, PA: Anderson and Meehan, 1818), Title page 1.

- Francis Wayland (Introductory Essay) in Eustace Carey, *Memoir of William Carey, D.D.: Late Missionary to Bengal; Professor of Oriental Languages in the College of Fort William, Calcutta* (Boston: Gould, Kendall and Lincoln, 1836), xvii.

- *Sixteenth Annual Report of the American Tract Society; Presented at New York, May 12, 1841: Showing the Progress of Tract Distribution and Visitation, Volume Circulation, and Foreign Distribution; With Evidences of the Divine Blessing, &c* (New York: Printed at the Society's House, by Daniel Fanshaw, 1841), 6.

- Taylor, John (compiler), *Biographical and Literary Notices of William Carey, D.D., The English Patriarch of Indian Missions and the First Professor of the Sanskrit and Other Oriental Languages in Indian Missions. Comprising Extracts from Church Books, Autograph MSS., and other Records. Also A List of Interesting Mementoes Connected with Carey. With Bibliographical Lists of Works relating to, or written by Carey; and pertaining to Baptist Missions in the East, etc. And Addenda* (Northampton: The Dryden Press, Taylor and Son; London: Alexander and Shepheard, 1886), Title page; Title page enlargement.

- Memorial Tablet to Carey from Harvey Lane Baptist Church, Leicester, England, Located in the William Carey Museum, Central Baptist Church, Leicester, England, UK.

Expect great things from God; [,] attempt great things for God.

- *Brief Narrative of the Baptist Mission in India: Including an Account of Translations of the Sacred Scriptures into the Various Languages of the East,* 5th ed. (London: Sold by Button & Son, 1819), 3.

APPENDIX

- Rev. Thomas Smith, *The History and Origin of the Missionary Societies*, Vol. I (London: Thos. Kelly and Richd. Evans, 1824), 317.

- Anderson, Christopher, *A Discourse Occasioned by the Death of the Rev. William Carey, D.D. of Serampore, Bengal, Delivered in Charlotte Chapel, on the Evening of 30th November 1834*, 2nd ed. (London: Parbury, Allen and Co., J. Nisbet, 1835).

- Eustace Carey, *Memoir of William Carey, D.D.: Late Missionary to Bengal; Professor of Oriental Languages in the College of Fort William, Calcutta*, with an Introductory Essay by Francis Wayland, D.D, President of Brown University (Boston: Gould, Kendall and Lincoln, 1836), 50.

- Baptist Missionary Society, William Carey Jubilee Medal, 1841, Obverse Reverse.

- Baptist Missionary Society, Jubilee, Anti-Slavery Medal, 1842.

- William Cathcart, ed., *The Baptist Encyclopedia*, 2 vols., rev. ed. (Philadelphia: Louis H. Everts, 1883), Vol. I, 182.

- Arthur C. Chute, *William Carey, A Sketch of Beginnings in Modern Missions*, prefatory note by Rev. E. B. Hulbert, D.D. (Chicago: Goodman & Dickerson, 1891), 24–25.

- Plaque Commemorating William Carey, Lower Circular Road Baptist Church, Calcutta.

- William Carey University, Hattiesburg, MS, USA.

- Carey Baptist College, University of Auckland, Auckland, New Zealand.

Expect great things from God. Attempt great things for God.

- Jeremiah Chaplin, "An Introductory Essay," in Eustace Carey, *Memoir of William Carey, D.D.: Late Missionary to Bengal; Professor of Oriental Languages in the College of Fort William, Calcutta. With an Introductory Essay by Francis Wayland, D.D., President of Brown University* (Hartford: Canfield and Robins, 1837), 18.

- John Brown Myers, ed., *The Centenary Volume of the Baptist Missionary Society 1792–1892* (London: The Baptist Missionary Society, 1892), Title page.

- George Smith, *The Life of William Carey, Shoemaker and Missionary* (London: Murray, 1887), ch. 2.

Expect great things from God, and attempt great things for God.

- John Overton Choules, "The Missionary a Contributor to Science and Literature," in *Christ's Messengers: Or, The Missionary Memorial*, ed. Edward Walker (New York: E. Walker, 1848), 330–331.

- Thomas Armitage, *A History of the Baptists; Traced by Their Vital Principles and Practices, from the Time of Our Lord and Saviour Jesus Christ to the Year 1886*, introduction by J. L. M. Curry (New York: Bryan, Taylor, & Co., 1887), 581.

Attempt great things for God and expect great things from God.

- Marianne Farningham, "The Shoemaker Missionary" [a poem], in *Friends' Review: A Religious, Literary and Miscellaneous Journal*, ed. Henry Hartshorne, Vol. XL (Philadelphia: Published at 1316 Filbert Street, 1886–1887), 607.

- Carey College, Sri Lanka.

- (Source: http://www.wmcarey.edu/carey/expect/).

Sources Cited

AAE: Walston, Vaughn J., and Robert J. Stevens. *African-American Experience in World Mission: A Call Beyond Community*. Pasadena, CA: William Carey Library, 2002.

AC: Amy Carmichael: http://www.goodreads.com/author/quotes/3935881.Amy_Wilson_Carmichael

ACD: Cocris, G. Michael. *Evangelism: A Biblical Approach*. Chicago: Moody Press, 1984.

AFC: Woodbridge, John D. *Ambassadors for Christ*. Chicago: Moody Press, 1994.

AG: Osbeck, Kenneth W. *Amazing Grace: 366 Inspiring Hymn Stories for Daily Devotions*. Grand Rapids, MI: Kregel Publications, 2002.

AJB: Broomhall, A. J. *Hudson Taylor and China's Open Century, Book Four: Survivors' Pact*. London: Hodder and Stoughton and Overseas Missionary Fellowship, 1984.

AJB1: Broomhall, A. J. *Hudson Taylor and China's Open Century, Book Two: Assault on the Nine*. London: Hodder and Stoughton and Overseas Missionary Fellowship, 1982.

AJB2: Broomhall, A. J. *Hudson Taylor and China's Open Century, Book Six: Over the Treaty Wall*. London: Hodder and Stoughton and Overseas Missionary Fellowship, 1988.

AM: Murray, Andrew. *The Key to the Missionary Problem: A Passionate Call to Obedience in Action*. Fort Washington, PA: CLC Publications, 1981.

SOURCES CITED

AM1: Murray, Andrew. *Humility.* New Kensington, PA: Whitaker House, 1982.

AMac: http://christianbookshelf.org/maclaren/expositions_of_holy_scripture_ephesians_peter/pleasing_christ.htm

AMG: Newell, Marvin J. *A Martyr's Grace.* Chicago: Moody Publishers, 2006.

AW: Walls, Andrew. *The Missionary Movement in Christian History.* Maryknoll, NY: Orbis Books, 2005.

B66: http://www2.wheaton.edu/bgc/archives/docs/Berlin66/Henry.htm

BAM: Johnson, C. Neal. *Business As Mission: A Comprehensive Guide To the Theory and Practice.* Downers Grove, IL: InterVarsity Press, 2009.

BB: http://bobblincoe.wordpress.com/2011/07/07/prayer-for-a-pastor-in-iraq/

BCWE: http://bcwe.org/2010/02/25/dr-oswald-j-smith/

BF: Taylor, Dr. and Mrs. Howard. *By Faith: Henry W. Frost and the China Inland Mission.* Singapore: OMF Books, 1988.

BG: http://thebillygrahamstory.com

BHK: Byang H. Kato, Urbana plenary address, 1970.

BMM: *"Missions: A Baptist Monthly Magazine."* Vol. VII, Boston, 1916.

BOY: Taylor, Mrs. Howard. *Borden of Yale.* Bloomington, MN: Bethany House Publishers, 1988.

BSWE: Biblical School of World Missions, www.bswe.org/resources/missions-quotes

BTH: http://belongtohim.xanga.com/521023739/item/

BTM: Peters, George W. *A Biblical Theology of Missions.* Chicago: Moody Press, 1972.

CCP: Lederleitner, Mary T. *Cross-Cultural Partnerships.* Downers Grove, IL: InterVarsity Press, 2010.

CCS: Elmer, Duane. *Cross-Cultural Servanthood: Serving the world in Christlike Humility.* Downers Grove, IL: IVP Books, 2006.

CD: http://www.teamworld.org/learn/people/team-international-director/6-intl-dir.html

CDI: http://www.teamworld.org/learn/people/team-international-director/123-international-directors-letter.html

CD2: Charlie Davis. *TEAM Horizons*, Issue 2, 2010.

CED: McGavran, Donald A. *The Conciliar-evangelical debate.* Pasadena, CA: William Carey Library, 1977.

CFU: Hunter, G. G. *Church of the Unchurched.* Nashville, TN: Abingdon, 1996.

CHI: Henry, Carl F. H. *Toward A Recovery of Christian Belief.* Wheaton, IL: Crossway Books, 1990.

CHS: Spurgeon, Charles H. *Beside Still Waters: Words of Comfort For The Soul.* Nashville, TN: Thomas Nelson Publishers, 1999.

CHSI: Spurgeon, Charles H. *The Gospel of the Kingdom.* C. H. Spurgeon, 1979 reprint.

CL: Christopher Little. *International Journal of Frontier Missiology*, April-June 2008.

CO: Calisto Odede of Kenya, Lausanne Address at Cape Town 2010.

COD: Bonhoeffer, Dietrich. *The Cost of Discipleship.* New York: Touchstone, 1995.

CP: Rev. Charles Price, People's Church, Toronto. Plenary address given at CrossGlobal Link/The Mission Exchange Personnel Conference, Rockville, VA, Dec. 2010.

CQ-AJ: http://christian-quotes.ochristian.com/Adoniram-Judson-Quotes/

CQR: christian-quotes.ochristian.com/Redemption-Quotes

SOURCES CITED

CRWM: http://www.crcna.org/pages/crwm_mee_prayerqts.cfm

CSL: Lewis, C. S. *Mere Christianity*. New York: HarperCollins, 1952.

CT: http://www.christianitytoday.com/moi/2000/005/october/26.26.html

CTC: *Cape Town Commitment*, Lausanne Movement. Bodmin, UK: Printbridge, 2011.

CTD: Estes, Steve. *Called to Die: The Story of American Linguist Chet Bitterman*. Grand Rapids, MI: Zondervan, 1986.

CTS: Studd, C. T. *Rescue Station at the Gates of Hell*. Also find at: http://www.thetravelingteam.org/articles/rescue-station-gates-hell

CTS1: Grubb, Norman P. *C.T. Studd: Cricketer and Pioneer*. London: Religious Tract Society, 1933.

CTV: *Catch the Vision: The Story of HCJB—The Voice of the Andes*. Opa Locka, FL: World Radio Missionary Fellowship, Inc., 1989.

CUTM: Neely, Lois. *Come Up to This Mountain: The Miracle of Clarence Jones & HCJB*. Wheaton, IL: Tyndale House Publishers, 1980.

CW: Christopher Wright, Cape Town 2010 plenary address.

CWJ: http://www.ccminternational.org/English/who_said_that/clarence%20jones.htm

DAC: Carson, D. A. *A Call to Spiritual Reformation: Priorities from Paul and His Prayers*. Grand Rapids, MI: Baker Book House, 1992.

DCQ: dailychristianquote.com/dcqfellowship5.html

DCQ-HT: http://dailychristianquote.com/dcqtaylor.html

DEH: http://www.archive.org/stream/TheInsightOfASeerD.E.Hoste/TheInsightOfASeer-D.E.Hoste_djvu.txt

DG: Henderson, Daniel. *Defying Gravity: How to Survive the Storms of Pastoral Ministry*. Chicago: Moody Publishers, 2010.

DH1: Hesselgrave, David J. Unpublished manuscript, "Will We Correct the 'Edinburg Error,'" 2010.

DH2: Hesselgrave, David J. *Planting Churches Cross-Culturally: North America and Beyond*. 2nd ed. Grand Rapids, MI: Baker Academic, 2000.

DLM: Moody, Dwight Layman. *Heaven: where it is, its inhabitants and how to get there*. Chicago: F. H. Revell, 1880.

DLM1: Moody, D. L. *To The Work! To The Work! Exhortations to Christians*. Chicago: F. H. Revell, 1884.

DR: David Ruiz, Associate Director, WEA, plenary address at Cape Town 2010.

EDWM: Moreau, A. Scott, editor. *Evangelical Dictionary of World Missions*. Grand Rapids, MI: Baker Books, 2000.

EEL: Elizabeth Elliot Leitch, Urbana plenary address, 1976. https://urbana.org/past-urbanas

EGK: Fortunak, Laurie Nichols, A. Scott Moreau, and Gary R. Corwin, eds. *Extending God's Kingdom: Church Planting Yesterday, Today, Tomorrow*. Wheaton, IL: EMIS, 2011.

EJ: Edward Judson, speaking of his father: http://www.biblebaptistelmont.org/BBC/library/judson.html

EJA: Eric J. Alexander, Urbana plenary address, 1981. https://urbana.org/past-urbanas

EL: Erwin Lutzer, Pastor Moody Church, given at ACMC conference, Oakbrook, IL, 2010.

EMB: Bounds, E. M. *The Complete Works of E. M. Bounds*. Radford, VA: Wilder Publications, 2008.

EMQ1: Payne, J. D. "Ethical Guidelines of Church Planters." *Evangelical Missions Quarterly*, January 2010, Vol. 46, No.1.

SOURCES CITED

EMQ2: Moreau, A. Scott. "A Word from the Editor." *Evangelical Missions Quarterly*, April 2009, Vol. 46, No. 2.

EMQ3: *Evangelical Missions Quarterly*, April 2003, Vol. 39, No. 2.

EMQ4: *Evangelical Missions Quarterly*, October 2002, Vol. 38, No. 4.

EMQ5: *Evangelical Missions Quarterly*, April 2004, Vol. 40, No. 2.

EMT: http://www.electrifying-mission-trips.org/Missionary-Quotes-2.html

ENRM: Hexam, Stephen Rost, and John Morehead. *Encountering New Religious Movements: A Holistic Approach*. Grand Rapids, MI: Kregel Publications, 2004.

ETM: Craig Ott, Stephen Strauss, with Timothy C. Tennent. *Encountering Theology of Mission*. Grand Rapids, MI: Baker Academic, 2010.

F&F: Walker, Jean, compiler. *Fool & Fanatic?* Bucks (UK) Worldwide Evangelization Crusade, 1980.

FLI: http://www.frontlineintercessors.ca/?page_id=27

FQC: www.finestquotes.com/quote_with-keyword-God-page-6.htm

FQ-PB: http://www.famousquotes.com/author/phillips-brooks/2

FUAC: Piper, John. *Filling Up the Afflictions of Christ: The Cost of Bringing the Gospel to the Nations in the Lives of William Tyndale, Adoniram Judson, and John Paton*. Wheaton, IL: Crossway Books, 2009.

FUT: Percy, J. O., ed. *Facing the Unfinished Task: Messages Delivered at the Congress on World Missions*. Grand Rapids, MI: Zondervan Publishing House, 1961.

FWCM: http://www.foundationscourse.org/

GDE: Robinson, Michael A. *God Does Exist! Defending the Faith Using Pre-suppositional Apologists*. Bloomington, IN: Author House, 2006.

GGC: Tucker, Ruth. *Guardians of The Great Commission*. Grand
Rapids, MI: The Zondervan Corporation, 1988.

GGD: http://www.greatergrace.ie/articles/57-mission-quotes.
html

GGWG: Presler, Titus Leonard. *Going Global With God: Reconciling
Mission in a World of Indifference*. Harrisburg, PA: Morehouse
Publishing, 2010.

GLC: Sanneh, Lamin. "The Gospel. Language, and Culture:
The Theological Method in Cultural Anaylsis."
International Review of Missions 84 (January–April).

GM: Thomson, A. *Great Missionaries: A Series of Biographies*. New
York: T. Nelson & Sons, 1862.

GMC: Taylor, William, ed. *Global Missiology for the 21st Century*.
Grand Rapids, MI: Baker Academic, 2000.

GMN: http://www.globalmissionsnetwork.info/flquotes.html

GMP: Van Engen, Charles. *God's Missionary People: Rethinking the
Purpose of the Local Church*. Grand Rapids, MI: Baker Book
House, 1991.

GRN: Colin Scott, *"Sounds of GRN,"* 2010.

GRN2: http://www.facebook.com/notes/
global-recordings-network/even-when-you-
must-do-it-byfaith/375368551686?comment_
id=12727834&offset=0&total_comments=1

GRQ: http://www.goodreads.com/quotes/

HB: Blackaby, Henry, and Richard Blackaby. *Experiencing God:
Knowing and Doing the Will of God*. Nashville, TN: B&H
Books, 2008.

HG: Guinness, Howard. (booklet) *Sacrifice*. 1939.

HIK: Goforth, Rosalind. *How I Know God Answers Prayer: The Personal
Testimony of One Lifetime*. Chicago: Moody Press, n.d.

SOURCES CITED

HM: History Makers: http://www.historymakers.info/stuff/resources.html

HT: Taylor, Dr. and Mrs. Howard. *Hudson Taylor & The China Inland Mission*. Philadelphia: China Inland Mission, 1955.

HTLD: Steer, Roger. *Hudson Taylor: Lessons on Discipleship*. OMF International, 1995.

HTSS: Taylor, Howard, and George Verwer. *Hudson Taylor's Spiritual Secret*. Chicago: Moody Publishers, 2009.

HV: Venn, Henry: "Instructions of the Committee of the Church Missionary Society of Departing Missionaries," June 30, 1868, reproduced in W. Knight, "The Missionary Secretariat of Henry Venn," 1880.

IFMA: Frazen, Edwin L. *75 Years of IFMA 1917–1992*. Pasadena, CA: William Carey Library, 1992.

ILC: Thomas, W. Ian. *The Indwelling Life of Christ: All of Him in All of Me*. Colorado Springs, CO: Multnomah Books, 2006.

IMB: http://www.imb.org/main/give/page.asp?StoryID=5530&LanguageID=1709

IMG: "Israel My Glory." Sept/Oct 2010.

ITG: Ahrend, Todd. *In This Generation*. Colorado Springs, CO: Dawson Media, 2010.

ITL: Tokunaga, Paul. *Invitation to Lead: Guidance for Emerging Asian American Leaders*. Downers Grove, IL: InterVarsity Press, 2003.

JCV: John C. Vockler, "Sermon at the Mass Meeting of Missionary Witness," included in Anglican Congress 1963: Report of Proceedings, Eugene Rathbone Fairweather, ed., Editorial Committee, Anglican Congress, 1963, pp. 148–49.

JCW: J. Christy Wilson, Urbana plenary, 1976. https://urbana.org/past-urbanas

JDB: Edwards, Jonathan. *Life and Journal of Rev. Dav. Brainerd*. James
    Duncan, 1835.

JDM: Fernando, Ajith. *Jesus Driven Ministry*. Wheaton, IL:
    Crossway Books, 2002.

JEJ: Personal journal of Jim Elliot, October 28, 1949, entry.

JHT: Taylor, J. Hudson. *The Works of J. Hudson Taylor*. Douglas
    Editions, 2009.

JHTR: Taylor, J. Hudson. *A Retrospect*. Philadelphia: China
    Inland Mission, n.d.

JIP: James I. Packer, "The Wrath of God," in *Evangelical Magazine*
    (1959).

JIP1: Packer, James I. *Evangelism and the Sovereignty of God*. England:
    Intervarsity Press, 1961.

JM: www.compassrose.org/contact.htm

JOC: John Overton Choules, "The Missionary a Contributor
    to Science and Literature," in Christ's Messengers: Or,
    The Missionary Memorial, ed. Edward Walker. New
    York: E. Walker, 1848.

JOF: Fraser, James O. "The Prayer of Faith." http://www.omf.
    org/omf/us/resources_1/prayer_resources/the_prayer_
    of_faith

JOS: Sanders, J. Oswald. *What of Those Who Have Never Heard?*
    Crowborough, East Sussex, UK: Highland Books, 1986.

JP1: John Piper, Lausanne plenary address at Cape Town 2010.

JP2: http://www.desiringgod.org/resource-library/taste-see-
    articles/ten-lessons-i-learned-from-my-father

JP3: http://www.goodreads.com/author/quotes/25423.John_
    Piper

JP4: Piper, John. *Bloodlines: Race, Cross, and the Christian*. Wheaton,
    IL: Crossway Books, 2011.

SOURCES CITED

JRM: Mott, John Raleigh. *The Evangelism of the World in This Generation*.
New York: Student Volunteer Movement, 1905.

JRS: The Report of the Toronto Convention (1902).

JS: John R. W. Stott, Urbana 1970 plenary address, https://
urbana.org/past-urbanas

JS1: John R. W. Stott, Urbana 1973 plenary address, https://
urbana.org/past-urbanas

JS2: John R. W. Stott, Urbana 1976 plenary address, https://
urbana.org/past-urbanas

JS3: John R. W. Stott, Urbana 1979 plenary address, https://
urbana.org/past-urbanas

JSGA: John Stam's Moody Bible Institute Graduation Address,
April 21, 1932, http://www2.wheaton.edu/bgc/archives/
docs/Stam/02.htm

JW: http://www.imarc.cc/buletins/wesleyq.html

KSL: Latourette, Kenneth Scott. *These Sought a Country*. New York:
Harper and Brothers, 1950.

KW: http://ponderanew.wordpress.com/2011/05/28/living-
out-a-missionary-heart/

LAC: Plueddemann, James. *Leading Across Cultures*. Downers
Grove, IL: IVP Academic, 2009.

LAI: Loritts, Crawford W. *Leadership As An Identity*. Chicago:
Moody Publishers, 2009.

LAJ: Judson, Edward. *The Life of Adoniram Judson*. New York: Anson
D. F. Randolph & Company, 1883.

LB: Lindsay Brown, Lausanne address at Cape Town 2010.

LCC: Lingenfelter, Sherwood G. *Leading Cross-Culturally: Covenant
Relationships for Effective Christian Leadership*. Grand Rapids, MI:
Baker Academic, 2008.

LDB: Edwards, Jonathan. *The Life of David Brainerd, Missionary to the Indians*. New York: The Christian Alliance Publishing Company, 1925.

LIR: http://lifeinreturn.wordpress.com/quotes/

LN1: Newbigin, Lesslie. *The Household of God*. SCM, 1953.

LNBG: Piper, John. *Let The Nations Be Glad*. Grand Rapids, MI: Baker Academic, 2004.

LSM: Savage, Robert. *Lord Send Me!* Grand Rapids, MI: Zondervan Publishing House, 1943.

LSS: Kitchen, John. *Long Story Short: God, Eternity, History and You*. Fort Washington, PA: CLC Publications, 2010.

LTC: Miley, George. *Loving the Church, Blessing the Nations*. Colorado Springs, CO: Biblica Publishing, 2003.

LTP: Matthews, Basil. *Livingstone the Pathfinder*. Missionary Movement of the United States and Canada, 1912.

MAE: Spurgeon, Charles. *Morning and Evening*. New Kensington, PA: Whitaker House, 2001.

MBI: Vincent, James. *The MBI Story*. Chicago: Moody Publishers, 2011.

MCI: http://missionscatalyst.net/?p=2293

MCC: Harrison, Eugene Myers. *Missionary Crusaders for Christ*, 1967.

MF1: http://www.missionfrontiers.org/issue/article/on-mission-with-god

MF2: www.missionfrontiers.org/issue/.../joining-the-discipleship-revolution Jan 1, 2011.

MFL: Brumberg, Joan Jacobs. *Mission for Life: The Story of the Family of Adoniram Judson, the Dramatic Events of the First American Foreign Mission, and the Course of Evangelical Religion in the Nineteenth Century*. New York: Free Press, 1980.

SOURCES CITED

MG: Griffiths, Michael. *Give Up Your Small Ambitions*. Chicago: Moody Press, 1976.

MGP: Wright, Christopher J. H. *The Mission of God's People*. Grand Rapids, MI: Zondervan, 2010.

MGSB: Steetzer, Ed, executive editor, and Philip Nation, general editor: *The Mission of God Study Bible*: 2012. Nashville, TN: Holman Bible Publishers, 2012.

MH: Horton, Michael. *The Gospel Commission: Recovering God's Strategy for Making Disciples*. Grand Rapids: Baker Books, 2011.

MHM: Sargent, John. *A Memoir of the Rev. Henry Martyn, B.D.* London: L. B. Seely & Sons, 1830.

MHMF: Walsh, Pakenham W. *Modern Heroes of the Mission Field*. New York: Thomas Wittaker Bible House, 1890.

MJN: Newell, Marvin J. *Commissioned: What Jesus Wants You to Know as You Go*. St. Charles, IL: ChurchSmart Resources, 2010.

ML: Michael Loftis, "The Heart of God at the Ends of the Earth," in *Message Magazine*, June 28, 2010.

ML1: http://www.abwe.org/news/article/the-mystery-of-gods-call/

MLLAJ: Wayland, Francis. *A Memoir of the Life and Labors of the Rev. Adoniram Judson*, Vol. 1. Boston: Phillips, Sampson and Company, 1853.

MM: Allan, Roland. *Missionary Methods: St. Paul's or Ours?* Grand Rapids, MI: Wm. B. Eerdmans Publishing Co., 1962.

MOE: Nilsen, Maria, as told to Paul H. Sheetz. *Malla Moe*. Chicago: Moody Bible Institute, 1956.

MOG: Wright, Christopher J. H. *The Mission of God: Unlocking the Bible's Grand Narrative*. Downers Gove, IL: IVP Academic, 2006.

MOM: Stiles, J. Mack. *Marks of the Messenger*. Downers Grove, IL: InterVarsity Press, 2010.

MPE: Coleman, Robert E. *The Master Plan of Evangelism.* Grand Rapids: Fleming H. Revell, 1993.

MRW: *Missionary Review of the World*, Vol. V, January to December, 1892.

MS: Barlow, Sanna Morrison. *Mountain Springs: The Story of Gospel Recordings in the Philippines.* Chicago: Moody Press, 1960.

MSC: Livingstone, William Pringle: *Mary Slessor of Calabar: Pioneer Missionary.* New York: Hodder and Stoughon, 1916.

MSG: Wheeler, S. Reginald. *A Man Sent from God: A Biography of Robert E. Speer.* Old Tappan, NJ: Fleming H. Revell Company, 1956.

MUFH1: http://utmost.org/partakers-of-his-suffering/

MUFH2: http://utmost.org/classic/it-is-the-lord-classic/

MWC: Carey, Eustace. *Memoir of William Carey, D.D.* London: Jackson and Walford, 1836.

NAMLC: Skye Jethani, Address given at North American Mission Leaders Conference, of CrossGlobal Link/The Mission Exchange, Phoenix, AZ, September 2011.

NCBC: http://newcbc.org/resources/church-blog/post/the-saddest-verse-in-the-bible

OBM: Hale, Thomas. *On Being a Missionary.* Pasadena, CA: William Carey Library, 1995.

OC: Chambers, Oswald. *My Utmost For His Highest.* Uhrichsville, Ohio: Barbour Publishing, 1993. (Jan. 18 entry)

OG: Guinness, Os. *The Call.* Nashville, Word Publishing, 1998.

OGCT: Guinness, Os. Lausanne Movement Cape Town 2010 address.

OMF: http://www.omf.org/omf/us/resources_1/omf_archives/famous_china_inland_mission_quotations/j_o_fraser

OMF1: http://www.omf.org/omf/breakthrough/fraser_the_lisu/about_james_o_fraser/the_prayer_of_faith_1

SOURCES CITED

PB: Borthwick, Paul, *Six Dangerous Questions to Transform Your View of the World*. Downers Grove, IL: InterVarsity Press, 1996.

P&C: Philips, James M., and Robert T. Coote. *Toward the Twenty-first Century in Christian Mission*. Grand Rapids, MI: Eerdmans Publishing Co., 1993.

PF1: Patrick Fung, Lausanne plenary address at Cape Town 2010.

PF2: Fung, Patrick. *Live to be Forgotten: D. E. Hoste*. Hong Kong: OMF, 2008.

PFI: Lyall, Leslie T. *A Passion for the Impossible: The Continuing Story of the Mission Hudson Taylor Began*. London: OMF Books, 1965.

PG: McCasland, David. *Pure Gold: A New Biography of the Olympic Champion Who Inspired Chariots of Fire*. Grand Rapids: Discovery House Publishers, 2001.

PGR: Ryken, Philip Graham. *King Solomon: The Temptations of Money, Sex and Power*. Wheaton: Crossway Books, 2011.

PMC: Stezler, Ed. *Planting Missional Churches*. Nashville: Broadman & Holman Publishers, 2006.

PMS: McClure, Rev. J. B. *Pearls from Many Seas*. Wheaton, IL: Van Kampen Press, 1951.

POF: Fraser, James O. *The Prayer of Faith*. Kent, England: Overseas Missionary Fellowship, 1958.

PR: Dillon, William P. *People Raising: A Practical Guide to Raising Funds*. Chicago: Moody Publishers, 2012.

PTP: Bounds, E. M. *Power Through Prayer*. New York: Cosimo, 2007.

PWCM: Winter, Ralph D. and Stephen C. Hawthorne. *Perspectives on the World Christian Movement*, 3rd ed. Pasadena: William Carey Library, 1999.

QB: quotationsbook.com/quote

QUO: http://www.quotes.net/quotations/place-worship

RAI: Ramez Atallah, Cape Town 2010 address.

RAD: Platt, David. *Radical*. Colorado Springs, CO: Multnomah Books, 2010.

RAQ: http://www.brainyquote.com/quotes/authors/r/roland_allen.html

RAT: Torrey, Ruben Archer. *How to Obtain Fullness of Power in Christian Life and Service*. Chicago: Fleming H. Revell Company, 1807.

R&T: Sills, David, *Reaching and Teaching*. Chicago: Moody Publishers, 2010.

RDW: Winter, Ralph, and Beth Snodderly. *Foundations of the World Christian Movement*. Pasadena, CA: Institute of International Studies, 2008.

RES: Robert E. Speer, "Are the Unevangelized Heathen Lost?" in *Sunday School Times*.

RF: http://www.reformationtheology.com/2006/06/if_sinners_will_be_damned.php

RFM: http://www.resourcesformissions.org/missions-quotes.html

RHG: Glover, Robert Hall. *The Bible Basis of Missions*. Los Angeles: Bible House of Los Angeles, 1946.

RHH: Hunt, Rosalie Hall. *Bless God and Take Courage: The Judson History and Legacy*. Valley Forge, PA: Judson Press, 2005.

RR: The Reform Reader: http://www.reformedreader.org/rbb/judson/biography05.htm

RTS: www.rts.edu/Site/Resources/.../RTSO_MDiv_Brochure.pdf

SC: Steve Coffey, http://www.devxtemp.info/joomla/index.php?option=com_content&view=article&id=244:christar&catid=65:associates-c&Itemid=66

SOURCES CITED

SEC: Allen, Roland. *The Spontaneous Expansion of the Church*. Grand Rapids, MI: Eerdmans, 1962.

SGA: http://www.sga.org/about/history/

SHT: The Spirituality of Hudson Taylor: http://ruach. wordpress.com/papers-written/the-spirituality-of-hudson-taylor/

SHY: Finnemore, William. *The Story of a Hundred Years: 1823–1923*. Oxford: At the University Press, 1923.

SJ: www.samueljohnson.com/charity.html

SL: Sanders, J. Oswald. *Spiritual Leadership*. Chicago: Moody Publishers, 2007.

SM: Murrary, Stuart. *Church Planting: Laying Foundations*. Scottdale, PA: Herald Press, 2001.

SMP: *Student Mission Power*. Pasadena, CA: William Carey Library, n.d.

SMZ: Zwemer, Samuel M. "The Glory of the Impossible." Princeton, NJ: *The Princeton Bulletin*, 1949.

SMZ1: Zwemer, Samuel Martinus. *The Unoccupied Mission Fields of Africa and Asia*.
New York: Student Volunteer Movement For Foreign Missions, 1911.

SMZ2: Zwemer, Samuel M. *Islam: A Challenge to Faith*. New York: Student Volunteer Movement for Foreign Missions, 1909.

SN: Neil, Stephen. "How My Mind Has Changed about Mission," video recording produced by Overseas Ministry Study Center, 1984.

SNU: Southern Nazarene University, http://home.snu.edu/~hculbert/slogans.htm, "Missions slogans and notable Quotes From Missionaries."

SOM: Burnett, Whit. *The Spirit Of Man*. New York: Hawthorn Books, Inc., 1958.

SPMC: *Students and the Present Missionary Crisis*. New York: Student Volunteer Movement, 1910.

SQB: Zuck, Roy. *The Speaker's Quote Book*. Grand Rapids, MI: Kregel Publications, 1997.

SS: Shadrach, Steve. *View Points: Fresh Perspectives on Personal Support Raising*. BodyBuilders Press, 2010.

SSS: http://sadhusundersinghfoundation.com/

STL: Harper, Keith, ed. *Send The Light: Lottie Moon's Letters and Other Writings*. Macon, GA: Mercer University Press, 2002.

STV: Shibley, David and Naomi. *The Smoke of a Thousand Villages … and Other Stories of Real Life Heroes of Faith*. Nashville, TN: Thomas Nelson Publishers, 1989.

SVM2: Shaw, Ryan, International Lead Facilitator, SVM2 in "Student Mission Catalyzer," February 2012.

TC: "The Continent," March 6, 1913, "Consecrating All to God."

TCFG: Dawson, John. *Taking Our Cities For God*. Lake Mary, FL: Creation House, 1989.

TCM: Batterson, Mark. *The Circle Maker: Praying Circles Around Your Biggest Dreams and Greatest Fears*. Grand Rapids, MI: Zondervan, 2011.

TCOD: Bonhoeffer, Dietrich. *The Cost of Discipleship*. New York: Macmillian Publishing Co. Inc., 1937.

TCW: Akin, Daniel L. *Ten Who Changed the World*. Nashville, TN: B&H Publishing Group, 2010.

TET: To Every Tribe, www.toeverytribe.com/missionquotes

TFI: Bradshaw, Malcolm R. *Torch For Islam*. London: OMF Books.

TFS: Edman, Raymond V. *They Found the Secret*. Grand Rapids, MI: Zondervan Publishing House, 1960.

SOURCES CITED

TG: Meroff, Debbie. *True Grit*. Tyrone, GA: Authentic Media, 2004.

TGC: Dowsett, Rose. *The Great Commission*. Grand Rapids, CA: Monarch Books, 2001.

TGE: Cate, Patrick O. *Through God's Eyes*. Pasadena, CA: William Carey Library, 2003.

TGO: McQuilkin, Robertson. *The Great Omission: A Biblical Basis for World Evangelism*. Waynesboro, GA: Authentic Media, 1984.

TGS: Anderson, Courtney. *To The Golden Shore: The Life of Adoniram Judson*. New York: Little Brown and Company, 1956.

THS: Graham, Billy. *The Holy Spirit: Activing God's Power in Your Life*. Nashville, TN: W. Publishing Group, 1978.

TM: Bosch, David J. *Transforming Mission*. Maryknoll, NY: Orbis Books, 1991.

TMC: Sills, David. *The Missionary Call*. Chicago: Moody Publishers, 2008.

TMM: *The Missionary Magazine*, Vol. 31. Boston: Missionary Rooms, 1851.

TMOM: Kane, J. Herbert. *The Making of a Missionary*, 2nd ed. Grand Rapids, MI: Baker Book House, 1987.

TMQ: http://www.tentmaker.org/Quotes/faithquotes.htm

TMTH: *Theory of Missions to the Heathen*. American Board of commissioners for Foreign Missions, 1812.

TO: Wurmbrand, Richard. *The Overcomers*. Orlando, FL: Bridge-Logos, 2006.

TPH: Murray, Iain. *The Puritan Hope*. Edinburgh, Scotland: Banner of Truth Trust, 1971.

TSH: Graham, Billy. *The Secret of Happiness*. Nashville, TN: Thomas Nelson, 2002.

TTJ: Jeremiah, David. *Turning Toward Joy*. Colorado Springs, CO: David C. Cook, 2006.

TTT: The Traveling Team, www.thetravelingteam.org/node/196

TUC: Tucker, Ruth A. *From Jerusalem to Irian Jaya: A Biographical History of Christian Missions.* Grand Rapids, MI: Zondervan, 2004.

TWTP: Duewel, Wesley L. *Touch The World Through Prayer.* Grand Rapids, MI: Zondervan, 1986.

UCG: McGavran, Donald Anderson. *Understanding Church Growth.* Grand Rapids, MI: Wm. B. Eerdmans Publishing Company, 1980.

UCM: Kane, J. Herbert. *Understanding Christian Missions.* Grand Rapids, MI: Baker Book House, 1974.

UV: Hefley, James and Marti. *Unstilled Voices.* Chappaqua, NY: Christian Herald Books, 1981.

VI: Newell, Marvin. *Visions.* July 2008, Vol. 59, No. 3.

VLM: Pollock, John. *Victims of the Long March.* Waco, TX: Word Books, 1970.

WB: Barclay, William. *The Gospel of John Volume 2.* Philadelphia: Westminster Press, 1975.

WBC: Wiersbe, Warren W. *The Wiersbe Bible Commentary: The Complete Bible.* Colorado Springs, CO: David C. Cook, 2007.

WC: Carey, S. Pierce. *William Carey.* London: The Wakeman Trust, 1993.

WCM: Walker, Deanville F. *William Carey: Missionary Pioneer and Statesman.* London: Student Christian Movement, 1926.

WE: Meyer, Daniel. *Witness Essentials: Evangelism That Makes Disciples.* Downers Grove, IL: IVP Connect, 2012.

WGD: Olson, C. Gordon. *What In The World Is God Doing?* Cedar Knolls, NJ: Global Gospel Publishers, 1988.

WHH: Corbett, Steve, and Brian Fikkert. *When Helping Hurts.* Chicago: Moody Publishers, 2009.

WHT: Taylor, J. Hudson. *The Works of J. Hudson Taylor,* 2009.

SOURCES CITED

WIM: Kirk, J. Andrew. *What Is Mission?* Minneapolis: Fortress Press, 2000.

WJE: Rogers, Henry. *The Works of Jonathan Edwards*, Vol. I. New York: Daniel Appleton and Co., 1835.

WMC: Deyoung, Kevin, and Greg Gilbert: *What is the Mission of the Church?* Wheaton, IL: Crossway, 2011.

WOQ: http://www.worldofquotes.com/author/ Emil+Brunner/1/index.html

WQO: Livingstone, W. P. *The White Queen of Okoyong: Mary Slessor.* London: Hodder & Stoughton, 1916.

WR: Kelly, Bob. *Worth Repeating: More Than 5000 Classic and Contemporary Quotes.* Grand Rapids, MI: Kregel Publications, 2003.

WS: Shenk, Wilbert R. *Changing Frontiers of Mission.* Maryknoll, NY: Orbis Books, 1999.

WSG: Mahaney, C. J., ed. *Why Small Groups? Together Toward Maturity.* Gaithersburg, MD: Sovereign Grace Ministries, 1996.

WW: http://www.wholesomewords.org/missions/bioslessor2.html

WW1: Warren Webster, Urbana 1967 plenary address, https:// urbana.org/past-urbanas

WW2: Warren Webster, Urbana 1970 plenary address, https:// urbana.org/past-urbanas

WWE: *World-Wide Evangelization: The Urgent Business of the Church.* New York: Student Volunteer Movement For Foreign Missions, 1902.

WWEL: Montgomery, Helen Barrett. *Western Women in Eastern Lands.* New York: The MacMillan Company, 1910.

WWP: Myers, Bryant L. *Walking With the Poor.* Maryknoll, NY: Orbis Books, 1999.

Index